READ TO SUCCEED

Strategies for Reading Comprehension

2

INTRODUCTION

Welcome to the latest in our series ***READ TO SUCCEED*** *— Strategies for Reading Comprehension*. This book is the second of two volumes in a program designed for learners wanting to advance their reading comprehension skills. The ability to read English easily and well is crucial for scoring high on exams such as GEPT, TOEIC, and TOEFL, and it is also a meaningful skill to have in today's competitive job market. This book gives learners a chance to develop skills while taking pleasure in reading at the same time.

READ TO SUCCEED *— Strategies for Reading Comprehension* will bring you a variety of up-to-date and interesting topics. Each lesson includes a main passage and related text. Lessons for ***READ TO SUCCEED*** *— Strategies for Reading Comprehension* come with concisely stated objectives about which reading and vocabulary skills English learners are meant to develop. We will help students learn to grasp the main point of a passage by skimming and scanning. We will also lay out different methods for drawing conclusions and making inferences, comparing and contrasting, and understanding the purpose for which a passage is written. Challenging points such as collocations, context clues, sentence patterns, and relevant grammar will be presented in a way that helps students to improve but does not overwhelm them.

As with the first book in our ***READ TO SUCCEED*** *— Strategies for Reading Comprehension* series, book two is divided into 12 units. We start by examining sibling science and the complex psychology surrounding birth order. From there, we move on to the health benefits of coffee. In Unit Three, "Basketball Fever," we take you through the history of the game and on to an in-depth look at the NBA's most exciting player, LeBron James. The next few units cover the environment, table manners, and fine dining as suggested by Michelin guidebooks. Then it's music and unique careers. The last few units have a decidedly global feel to them. We talk about the oceans' rising levels and the islands this affects, then we travel to the Seven Wonders of the World. We close ***READ TO SUCCEED*** *— Strategies for Reading Comprehension* by looking at genetic modification. What do you say? Are you willing to eat this stuff?

Whether this is your first time with ***READ TO SUCCEED*** *— Strategies for Reading Comprehension* or you're carrying on from our first book, we're glad to have you. There's a lot to do and explore, so let's get started.

CONTENTS

CORPORATE DEVELOPMENT
PRACTICAL COURSE

CONTENT CHART

LEARNING OVERVIEW

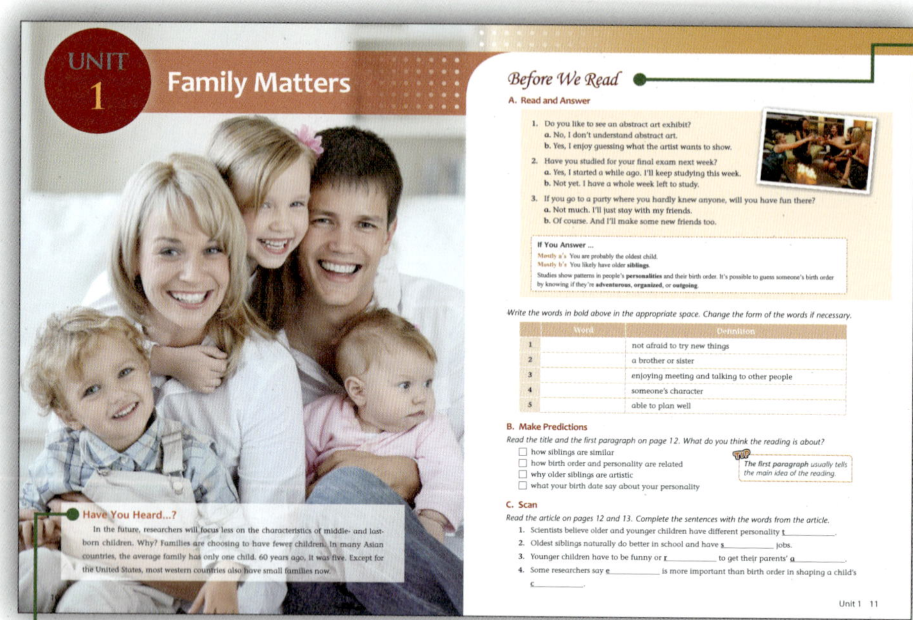
UNIT 1 Family Matters

Have You Heard...?

In the future, researchers will focus less on the characteristics of middle- and last-born children. Why? Families are choosing to have fewer children. In many Asian countries, the average family has only one child. 60 years ago, it was five. Except for the United States, most western countries also have small families now.

Before We Read

A. Read and Answer

1. Do you like to see an abstract art exhibit?
   a. No, I don't understand abstract art.
   b. Yes, I enjoy guessing what the artist wants to show.
2. Have you studied for your final exam next week?
   a. Yes, I started a while ago. I'll keep studying this week.
   b. Not yet. I have a whole week left to study.
3. If you go to a party where you hardly knew anyone, will you have fun there?
   a. Not much. I'll just stay with my friends.
   b. Of course. And I'll make some new friends too.

If You Answer ...

Studies show patterns in people's **personalities** and their birth order. It's possible to guess someone's birth order by knowing if they're **adventurous**, **organized**, or **outgoing**.

Write the words in bold above in the appropriate space. Change the form of the words if necessary.

	Word	Definition
1		not afraid to try new things
2		a brother or sister
3		enjoying meeting and talking to other people
4		someone's character
5		able to plan well

B. Make Predictions

Read the title and the first paragraph on page 12. What do you think the reading is about?

- ☐ how siblings are similar
- ☐ how birth order and personality are related
- ☐ why older siblings are artistic
- ☐ what your birth date say about your personality

The first paragraph usually tells the main idea of the reading.

C. Scan

Read the article on pages 12 and 13. Complete the sentences with the words from the article.

1. Scientists believe older and younger children have different personality t________.
2. Oldest siblings naturally do better in school and have s________ jobs.
3. Younger children have to be funny or r________ to get their parents' a________.
4. Some researchers say e________ is more important than birth order in shaping a child's c________.

Unit 1 11

Before We Read
provides background knowledge on the topic through short readings and various activities. Students can scan the main reading passage and prepare for the lesson.

THINK ABOUT IT
provides a relevant image and questions for students. The questions help students focus on the topic and stimulate their prior knowledge about the topic.

Comprehension Check
asks students about the topic, main idea, and details of the main passage. Students can check their understanding of the passage through diverse tasks, including Fill in the Blanks, Classification, True or False, and Multiple Choice, etc.

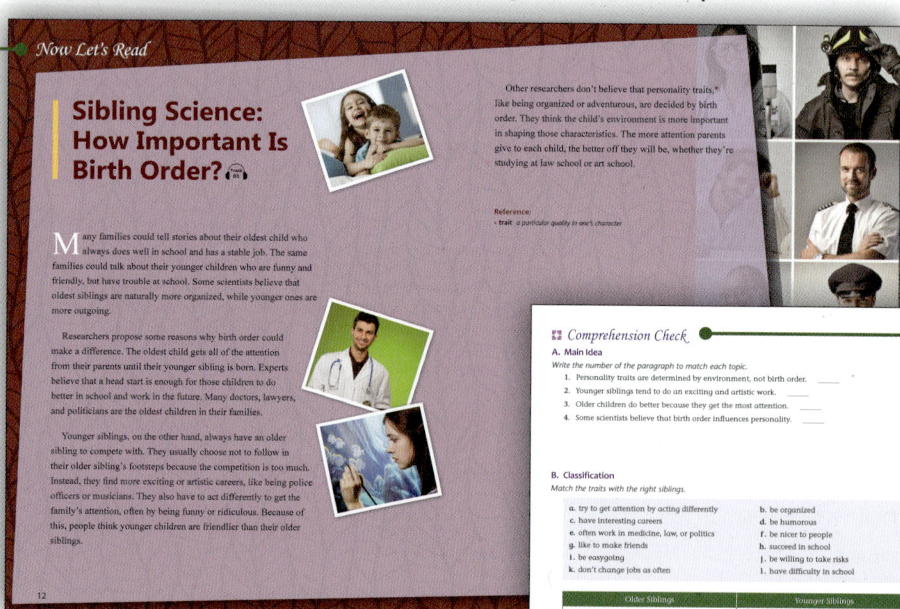
Now Let's Read

Sibling Science: How Important Is Birth Order?

Many families could tell stories about their oldest child who always does well in school and has a stable job. The same families could talk about their younger children who are funny and friendly, but have trouble at school. Some scientists believe that oldest siblings are naturally more organized, while younger ones are more outgoing.

Researchers propose some reasons why birth order could make a difference. The oldest child gets all of the attention from their parents until their younger sibling is born. Experts believe that a head start is enough for those children to do better in school and work in the future. Many doctors, lawyers, and politicians are the oldest children in their families.

Younger siblings, on the other hand, always have an older sibling to compete with. They usually choose not to follow in their older sibling's footsteps because the competition is too much. Instead, they find more exciting or artistic careers, like being police officers or musicians. They also have to act differently to get the family's attention, often by being funny or ridiculous. Because of this, people think younger children are friendlier than their older siblings.

Other researchers don't believe that personality traits,* like being organized or adventurous, are decided by birth order. They think the child's environment is more important in shaping those characteristics. The more attention parents give to each child, the better off they will be, whether they're studying at law school or art school.

Reference:
- trait a particular quality in one's character

12

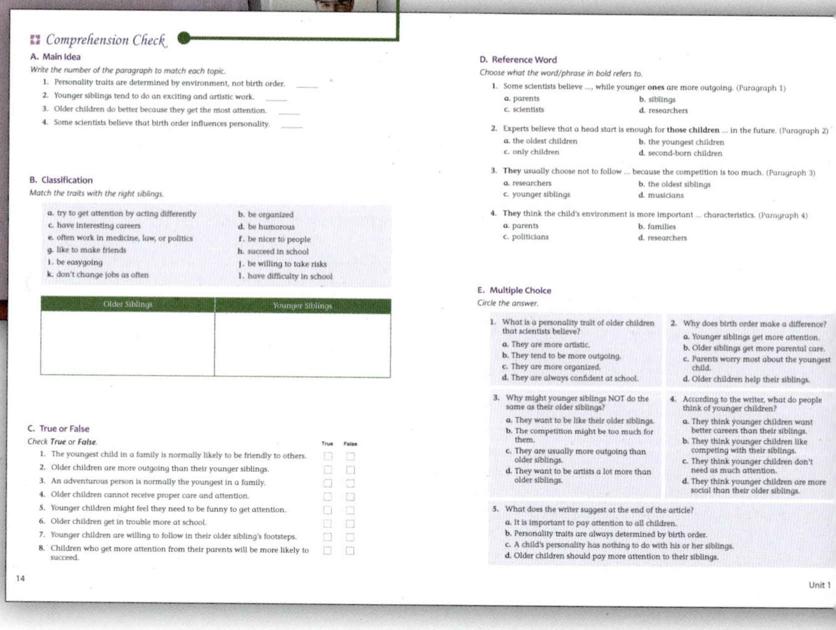
Comprehension Check

A. Main Idea

Write the number of the paragraph to match each topic.

1. Personality traits are determined by environment, not birth order. ____
2. Younger siblings tend to do an exciting and artistic work. ____
3. Older children do better because they get the most attention. ____
4. Some scientists believe that birth order influences personality. ____

B. Classification

Match the traits with the right siblings.

a. try to get attention by acting differently	b. be organized
c. have interesting careers	d. be humorous
e. often work in medicine, law, or politics	f. be nicer to people
g. like to make friends	h. succeed in school
i. be easygoing	j. be willing to take risks
k. don't change jobs as often	l. have difficulty in school

Older Siblings	Younger Siblings

C. True or False

Check True or False.

		True	False
1.	The youngest child in a family is normally likely to be friendly to others.	☐	☐
2.	Older children are more outgoing than their younger siblings.	☐	☐
3.	An adventurous person is normally the youngest in a family.	☐	☐
4.	Older children cannot receive proper care and attention.	☐	☐
5.	Younger children might feel they need to be funny to get attention.	☐	☐
6.	Older children get in trouble more at school.	☐	☐
7.	Younger children are willing to follow in their older sibling's footsteps.	☐	☐
8.	Children who get more attention from their parents will be more likely to succeed.	☐	☐

14

D. Reference Word

Choose what the word/phrase in bold refers to.

1. Some scientists believe ..., while younger **ones** are more outgoing. (Paragraph 1)
   a. parents b. siblings c. scientists d. researchers
2. Experts believe that a head start is enough for **those children** ... in the future. (Paragraph 2)
   a. the oldest children b. the youngest children c. only children d. second-born children
3. **They** usually choose not to follow ... because the competition is too much. (Paragraph 3)
   a. researchers b. the oldest siblings c. younger siblings d. musicians
4. **They** think the child's environment is more important ... characteristics. (Paragraph 4)
   a. parents b. families c. politicians d. researchers

E. Multiple Choice

Circle the answer.

1. What is a personality trait of older children that scientists believe?
   a. They are more artistic.
   b. They tend to be more outgoing.
   c. They are more organized.
   d. They are always confident at school.
2. Why does birth order make a difference?
   a. Younger siblings get more attention.
   b. Older siblings get more parental care.
   c. Parents worry most about the youngest child.
   d. Older children help their siblings.
3. Why might younger siblings NOT do the same as their older siblings?
   a. They want to be like their older siblings.
   b. The competition might be too much for them.
   c. They are usually more outgoing than older siblings.
   d. They want to be artists a lot more than older siblings.
4. According to the writer, what do people think of younger children?
   a. They think younger children want better careers than their siblings.
   b. They think younger children like competing with their siblings.
   c. They think younger children don't need as much attention.
   d. They think younger children are more social than their older siblings.
5. What does the writer suggest at the end of the article?
   a. It is important to pay attention to all children.
   b. Personality traits are always determined by birth order.
   c. A child's personality has nothing to do with his or her siblings.
   d. Older children should pay more attention to their siblings.

Unit 1

Now Let's Read
presents captivating articles to students. Students read about topics that interest them, including facts about people, animals, places, things and events, which enable them to broaden their knowledge as well.

Vocabulary Check
reaffirms students' knowledge of the key words and helps students build up their vocabulary.

Reading Strategy
provides reading strategies in each unit. Students can study Comparing and Contrasting, Drawing Conclusions, Making Inferences, Paraphrasing, and so on.

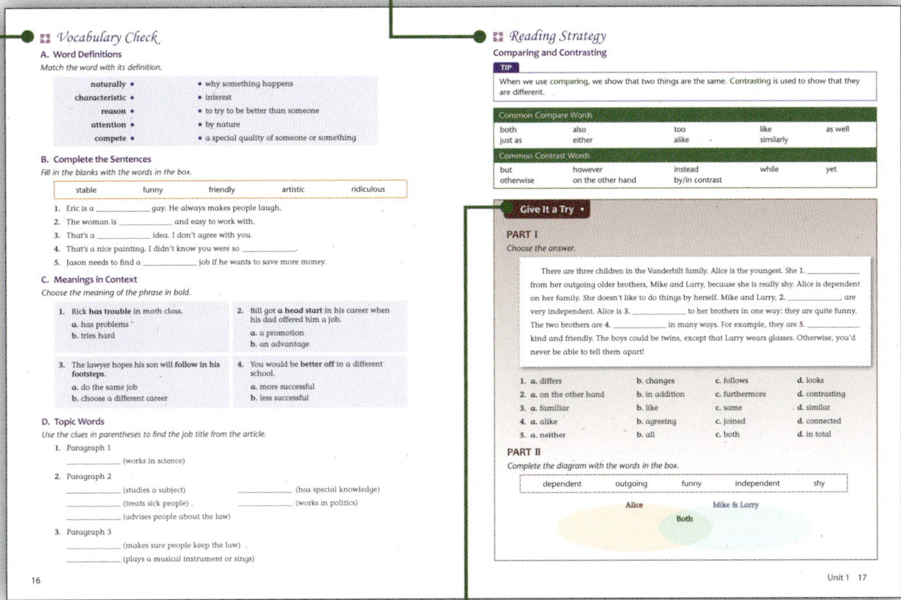

Vocabulary Check

A. Word Definitions
Match the word with its definition.

naturally • • why something happens
characteristic • • interest
reason • • to try to be better than someone
attention • • by nature
compete • • a special quality of someone or something

B. Complete the Sentences
Fill in the blanks with the words in the box.

stable	funny	friendly	artistic	ridiculous

1. Eric is a ________ guy. He always makes people laugh.
2. The woman is ________ and easy to work with.
3. That's a ________ idea. I don't agree with you.
4. That's a nice painting. I didn't know you were so ________.
5. Jason needs to find a ________ job if he wants to save more money.

C. Meanings in Context
Choose the meaning of the phrase in bold.

1. Rick **has trouble** in math class.
a. has problems
b. tries hard

2. Bill got **a head start** in his career when his dad offered him a job.
a. a promotion
b. an advantage

3. The lawyer hopes his son will **follow in his footsteps**.
a. do the same job
b. choose a different career

4. You would be **better off** in a different school.
a. more successful
b. less successful

D. Topic Words
Use the clues in parentheses to find the job title from the article.

1. Paragraph 1
________ (works in science)
2. Paragraph 2
________ (studies a subject) ________ (has special knowledge)
________ (treats sick people) ________ (works in politics)
________ (advises people about the law)
3. Paragraph 3
________ (makes sure people keep the law)
________ (plays a musical instrument or sings)

16

Reading Strategy
Comparing and Contrasting

TIP
When we use comparing, we show that two things are the same. Contrasting is used to show that they are different.

Common Compare Words				
both	also	too	like	as well
just as	either	alike	similarly	

Common Contrast Words				
but	however	instead	while	yet
otherwise	on the other hand	by/in contrast		

Give It a Try

PART I
Choose the answer.

There are three children in the Vanderbilt family. Alice is the youngest. She 1. ________ from her outgoing older brothers, Mike and Larry, because she is really shy. Alice is dependent on her family. She doesn't like to do things by herself. Mike and Larry, 2. ________, are very independent. Alice is 3. ________ to her brothers in one way: they are quite funny. The two brothers are 4. ________ in many ways. For example, they are 5. ________ kind and friendly. The boys could be twins, except that Larry wears glasses. Otherwise, you'd never be able to tell them apart!

1. a. differs b. changes c. follows d. looks
2. a. on the other hand b. in addition c. furthermore d. contrasting
3. a. familiar b. like c. same d. similar
4. a. alike b. agreeing c. joined d. connected
5. a. neither b. all c. both d. in total

PART II
Complete the diagram with the words in the box.

dependent	outgoing	funny	independent	shy

Unit 1 17

Give It a Try
provides an opportunity to practice the *Reading Strategy*. Students can verify their understanding of each unit's reading strategy.

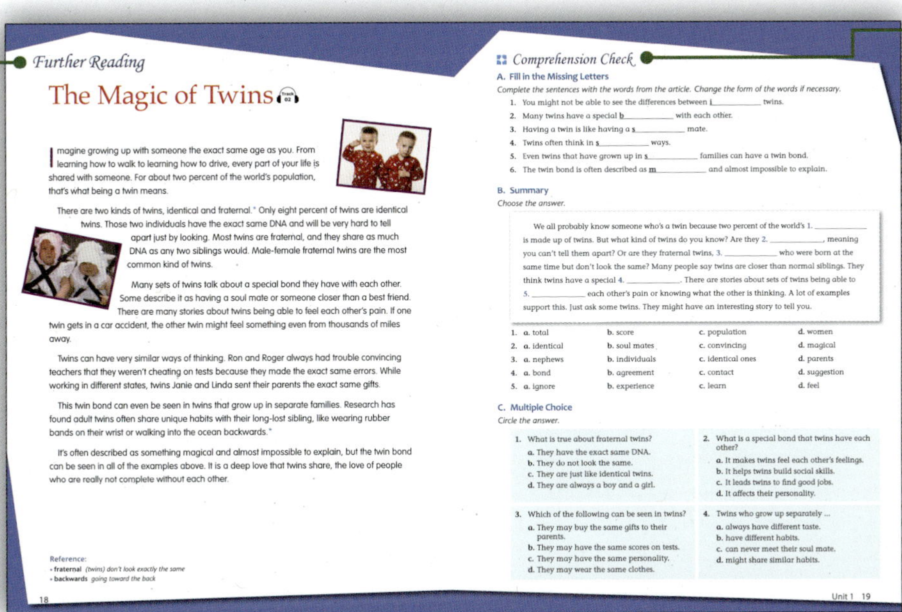

Further Reading

The Magic of Twins

Imagine growing up with someone the exact same age as you. From learning how to walk to learning how to drive, every part of your life is shared with someone. For about two percent of the world's population, that's what being a twin means.

There are two kinds of twins, identical and fraternal.* Only eight percent of twins are identical twins. Those two individuals have the exact same DNA and will be very hard to tell apart just by looking. Most twins are fraternal, and they share as much DNA as any two siblings would. Male-female fraternal twins are the most common kind of twins.

Many sets of twins talk about a special bond they have with each other. Some describe it as having a soul mate or someone closer than a best friend. There are many stories about twins being able to feel each other's pain. If one twin gets in a car accident, the other twin might feel something even from thousands of miles away.

Twins can have very similar ways of thinking. Ron and Roger always had trouble convincing teachers that they weren't cheating on tests because they made the exact same errors. While working in different states, twins Janie and Linda sent their parents the exact same gifts.

This twin bond can even be seen in twins that grow up in separate families. Research has found adult twins often share unique habits with their long-lost sibling, like wearing rubber bands on their wrist or walking into the ocean backwards.*

It's often described as something magical and almost impossible to explain, but the twin bond can be seen in all of the examples above. It is a deep love that twins share, the love of people who are really not complete without each other.

Reference:
• fraternal (twins) don't look exactly the same
• backwards going toward the back

18

Comprehension Check

A. Fill in the Missing Letters
Complete the sentences with the words from the article. Change the form of the words if necessary.

1. You might not be able to see the differences between i________ twins.
2. Many twins have a special b________ with each other.
3. Having a twin is like having a s________ mate.
4. Twins often think in s________ ways.
5. Even twins that have grown up in s________ families can have a twin bond.
6. The twin bond is often described as m________ and almost impossible to explain.

B. Summary
Choose the answer.

We all probably know someone who's a twin because two percent of the world's 1. ________ is made up of twins. But what kind of twins do you know? Are they 2. ________, meaning you can't tell them apart? Or are they fraternal twins, 3. ________ who were born at the same time but don't look the same? Many people say twins are closer than normal siblings. They think twins have a special 4. ________. There are stories about sets of twins being able to 5. ________ each other's pain or knowing what the other is thinking. A lot of examples support this. Just ask some twins. They might have an interesting story to tell you.

1. a. total b. score c. population d. women
2. a. identical b. soul mates c. convincing d. magical
3. a. nephews b. individuals c. identical ones d. parents
4. a. bond b. agreement c. contact d. suggestion
5. a. ignore b. experience c. learn d. feel

C. Multiple Choice
Circle the answer.

1. What is true about fraternal twins?
a. They have the exact same DNA.
b. They do not look the same.
c. They are just like identical twins.
d. They are always a boy and a girl.

2. What is a special bond that twins have each other?
a. It makes twins feel each other's feelings.
b. It helps twins build social skills.
c. It leads twins to find good jobs.
d. It affects their personality.

3. Which of the following can be seen in twins?
a. They may buy the same gifts to their parents.
b. They may have the same scores on tests.
c. They may have the same personality.
d. They may wear the same clothes.

4. Twins who grow up separately ...
a. always have different taste.
b. have different habits.
c. can never meet their soul mate.
d. might share similar habits.

Unit 1 19

Comprehension Check
checks students' understanding of *Further Reading* through a variety of exercises.

Further Reading
presents an extended reading passage related to the main reading passage. Students can polish their reading skill through this extra passage.

UNIT 1 Family Matters

Have You Heard...?

In the future, researchers will focus less on the characteristics of middle- and last-born children. Why? Families are choosing to have fewer children. In many Asian countries, the average family has only one child. 60 years ago, it was five. Except for the United States, most western countries also have small families now.

Before We Read

A. Read and Answer

1. Do you like to see an abstract art exhibit?
   a. No, I don't understand abstract art.
   b. Yes, I enjoy guessing what the artist wants to show.
2. Have you studied for your final exam next week?
   a. Yes, I started a while ago. I'll keep studying this week.
   b. Not yet. I have a whole week left to study.
3. If you go to a party where you hardly knew anyone, will you have fun there?
   a. Not much. I'll just stay with my friends.
   b. Of course. And I'll make some new friends too.

If You Answer ...

Mostly a's You are probably the oldest child.
Mostly b's You likely have older **siblings**.

Studies show patterns in people's **personalities** and their birth order. It's possible to guess someone's birth order by knowing if they're **adventurous**, **organized**, or **outgoing**.

Write the words in bold above in the appropriate space. Change the form of the words if necessary.

	Word	Definition
1		not afraid to try new things
2		a brother or sister
3		enjoying meeting and talking to other people
4		someone's character
5		able to plan well

B. Make Predictions

Read the title and the first paragraph on page 12. What do you think the reading is about?

- ☐ how siblings are similar
- ☐ how birth order and personality are related
- ☐ why older siblings are artistic
- ☐ what your birth date say about your personality

TIP ***The first paragraph*** *usually tells the main idea of the reading.*

C. Scan

Read the article on pages 12 and 13. Complete the sentences with the words from the article.

1. Scientists believe older and younger children have different personality **t**____________.
2. Oldest siblings naturally do better in school and have **s**____________ jobs.
3. Younger children have to be funny or **r**____________ to get their parents' **a**____________.
4. Some researchers say **e**____________ is more important than birth order in shaping a child's **c**____________.

Sibling Science: How Important Is Birth Order?

Track 01

Many families could tell stories about their oldest child who always does well in school and has a stable job. The same families could talk about their younger children who are funny and friendly, but have trouble at school. Some scientists believe that oldest siblings are naturally more organized, while younger ones are more outgoing.

Researchers propose some reasons why birth order could make a difference. The oldest child gets all of the attention from their parents until their younger sibling is born. Experts believe that a head start is enough for those children to do better in school and work in the future. Many doctors, lawyers, and politicians are the oldest children in their families.

Younger siblings, on the other hand, always have an older sibling to compete with. They usually choose not to follow in their older sibling's footsteps because the competition is too much. Instead, they find more exciting or artistic careers, like being police officers or musicians. They also have to act differently to get the family's attention, often by being funny or ridiculous. Because of this, people think younger children are friendlier than their older siblings.

Other researchers don't believe that personality traits,* like being organized or adventurous, are decided by birth order. They think the child's environment is more important in shaping those characteristics. The more attention parents give to each child, the better off they will be, whether they're studying at law school or art school.

Reference:

* **trait** *a particular quality in one's character*

Comprehension Check

A. Main Idea

Write the number of the paragraph to match each topic.

1. Personality traits are determined by environment, not birth order. ______
2. Younger siblings tend to do an exciting and artistic work. ______
3. Older children do better because they get the most attention. ______
4. Some scientists believe that birth order influences personality. ______

B. Classification

Match the traits with the right siblings.

a. try to get attention by acting differently
b. be organized
c. have interesting careers
d. be humorous
e. often work in medicine, law, or politics
f. be nicer to people
g. like to make friends
h. succeed in school
i. be easygoing
j. be willing to take risks
k. don't change jobs as often
l. have difficulty in school

Older Siblings	Younger Siblings

C. True or False

*Check **True** or **False**.*

	True	False
1. The youngest child in a family is normally likely to be friendly to others.	☐	☐
2. Older children are more outgoing than their younger siblings.	☐	☐
3. An adventurous person is normally the youngest in a family.	☐	☐
4. Older children cannot receive proper care and attention.	☐	☐
5. Younger children might feel they need to be funny to get attention.	☐	☐
6. Older children get in trouble more at school.	☐	☐
7. Younger children are willing to follow in their older sibling's footsteps.	☐	☐
8. Children who get more attention from their parents will be more likely to succeed.	☐	☐

D. Reference Word

Choose what the word/phrase in bold refers to.

1. Some scientists believe ..., while younger **ones** are more outgoing. (Paragraph 1)
   a. parents b. siblings
   c. scientists d. researchers

2. Experts believe that a head start is enough for **those children** ... in the future. (Paragraph 2)
   a. the oldest children b. the youngest children
   c. only children d. second-born children

3. **They** usually choose not to follow ... because the competition is too much. (Paragraph 3)
   a. researchers b. the oldest siblings
   c. younger siblings d. musicians

4. **They** think the child's environment is more important ... characteristics. (Paragraph 4)
   a. parents b. families
   c. politicians d. researchers

E. Multiple Choice

Circle the answer.

1. What is a personality trait of older children that scientists believe?
   a. They are more artistic.
   b. They tend to be more outgoing.
   c. They are more organized.
   d. They are always confident at school.

2. Why does birth order make a difference?
   a. Younger siblings get more attention.
   b. Older siblings get more parental care.
   c. Parents worry most about the youngest child.
   d. Older children help their siblings.

3. Why might younger siblings NOT do the same as their older siblings?
   a. They want to be like their older siblings.
   b. The competition might be too much for them.
   c. They are usually more outgoing than older siblings.
   d. They want to be artists a lot more than older siblings.

4. According to the writer, what do people think of younger children?
   a. They think younger children want better careers than their siblings.
   b. They think younger children like competing with their siblings.
   c. They think younger children don't need as much attention.
   d. They think younger children are more social than their older siblings.

5. What does the writer suggest at the end of the article?
   a. It is important to pay attention to all children.
   b. Personality traits are always determined by birth order.
   c. A child's personality has nothing to do with his or her siblings.
   d. Older children should pay more attention to their siblings.

Vocabulary Check

A. Word Definitions

Match the word with its definition.

naturally •	• why something happens
characteristic •	• interest
reason •	• to try to be better than someone
attention •	• by nature
compete •	• a special quality of someone or something

B. Complete the Sentences

Fill in the blanks with the words in the box.

stable	funny	friendly	artistic	ridiculous

1. Eric is a ______________ guy. He always makes people laugh.
2. The woman is ______________ and easy to work with.
3. That's a ______________ idea. I don't agree with you.
4. That's a nice painting. I didn't know you were so ______________.
5. Jason needs to find a ______________ job if he wants to save more money.

C. Meanings in Context

Choose the meaning of the phrase in bold.

1. Rick **has trouble** in math class.
   a. has problems
   b. tries hard

2. Bill got **a head start** in his career when his dad offered him a job.
   a. a promotion
   b. an advantage

3. The lawyer hopes his son will **follow in his footsteps.**
   a. do the same job
   b. choose a different career

4. You would be **better off** in a different school.
   a. more successful
   b. less successful

D. Topic Words

Use the clues in parentheses to find the job title from the article.

1. Paragraph 1

   ______________ (works in science)

2. Paragraph 2

   ______________ (studies a subject)
   ______________ (treats sick people)
   ______________ (advises people about the law)
   ______________ (has special knowledge)
   ______________ (works in politics)

3. Paragraph 3

   ______________ (makes sure people keep the law)
   ______________ (plays a musical instrument or sings)

Reading Strategy

Comparing and Contrasting

TIP

When we use comparing, we show that two things are the same. Contrasting is used to show that they are different.

Common Compare Words				
both	also	too	like	as well
just as	either	alike	similarly	

Common Contrast Words				
but	however	instead	while	yet
otherwise	on the other hand	by/in contrast		

• Give It a Try •

PART I

Choose the answer.

There are three children in the Vanderbilt family. Alice is the youngest. She **1.** ______________ from her outgoing older brothers, Mike and Larry, because she is really shy. Alice is dependent on her family. She doesn't like to do things by herself. Mike and Larry, **2.** ______________, are very independent. Alice is **3.** ______________ to her brothers in one way: they are quite funny. The two brothers are **4.** ______________ in many ways. For example, they are **5.** ______________ kind and friendly. The boys could be twins, except that Larry wears glasses. Otherwise, you'd never be able to tell them apart!

1. **a.** differs	**b.** changes	**c.** follows	**d.** looks
2. **a.** on the other hand	**b.** in addition	**c.** furthermore	**d.** contrasting
3. **a.** familiar	**b.** like	**c.** same	**d.** similar
4. **a.** alike	**b.** agreeing	**c.** joined	**d.** connected
5. **a.** neither	**b.** all	**c.** both	**d.** in total

PART II

Complete the diagram with the words in the box.

dependent	outgoing	funny	independent	shy

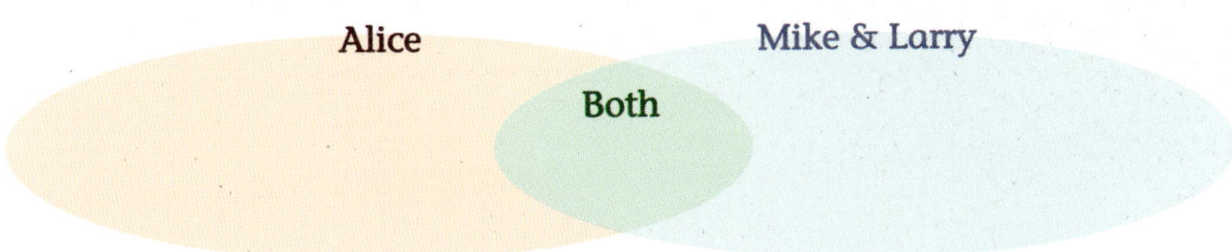

Further Reading

The Magic of Twins

Track 02

Imagine growing up with someone the exact same age as you. From learning how to walk to learning how to drive, every part of your life is shared with someone. For about two percent of the world's population, that's what being a twin means.

There are two kinds of twins, identical and fraternal.* Only eight percent of twins are identical twins. Those two individuals have the exact same DNA and will be very hard to tell apart just by looking. Most twins are fraternal, and they share as much DNA as any two siblings would. Male-female fraternal twins are the most common kind of twins.

Many sets of twins talk about a special bond they have with each other. Some describe it as having a soul mate or someone closer than a best friend. There are many stories about twins being able to feel each other's pain. If one twin gets in a car accident, the other twin might feel something even from thousands of miles away.

Twins can have very similar ways of thinking. Ron and Roger always had trouble convincing teachers that they weren't cheating on tests because they made the exact same errors. While working in different states, twins Janie and Linda sent their parents the exact same gifts.

This twin bond can even be seen in twins that grow up in separate families. Research has found adult twins often share unique habits with their long-lost sibling, like wearing rubber bands on their wrist or walking into the ocean backwards.*

It's often described as something magical and almost impossible to explain, but the twin bond can be seen in all of the examples above. It is a deep love that twins share, the love of people who are really not complete without each other.

Reference:

* **fraternal** *(twins) don't look exactly the same*
* **backwards** *going toward the back*

Comprehension Check

A. Fill in the Missing Letters

Complete the sentences with the words from the article. Change the form of the words if necessary.

1. You might not be able to see the differences between **i**__________ twins.
2. Many twins have a special **b**__________ with each other.
3. Having a twin is like having a **s**__________ mate.
4. Twins often think in **s**__________ ways.
5. Even twins that have grown up in **s**__________ families can have a twin bond.
6. The twin bond is often described as **m**__________ and almost impossible to explain.

B. Summary

Choose the answer.

We all probably know someone who's a twin because two percent of the world's 1. __________ is made up of twins. But what kind of twins do you know? Are they 2. __________, meaning you can't tell them apart? Or are they fraternal twins, 3. __________ who were born at the same time but don't look the same? Many people say twins are closer than normal siblings. They think twins have a special 4. __________. There are stories about sets of twins being able to 5. __________ each other's pain or knowing what the other is thinking. A lot of examples support this. Just ask some twins. They might have an interesting story to tell you.

	a	b	c	d
1.	**a.** total	**b.** score	**c.** population	**d.** women
2.	**a.** identical	**b.** soul mates	**c.** convincing	**d.** magical
3.	**a.** nephews	**b.** individuals	**c.** identical ones	**d.** parents
4.	**a.** bond	**b.** agreement	**c.** contact	**d.** suggestion
5.	**a.** ignore	**b.** experience	**c.** learn	**d.** feel

C. Multiple Choice

Circle the answer.

1. What is true about fraternal twins?
   - **a.** They have the exact same DNA.
   - **b.** They do not look the same.
   - **c.** They are just like identical twins.
   - **d.** They are always a boy and a girl.

2. What is a special bond that twins have each other?
   - **a.** It makes twins feel each other's feelings.
   - **b.** It helps twins build social skills.
   - **c.** It leads twins to find good jobs.
   - **d.** It affects their personality.

3. Which of the following can be seen in twins?
   - **a.** They may buy the same gifts to their parents.
   - **b.** They may have the same scores on tests.
   - **c.** They may have the same personality.
   - **d.** They may wear the same clothes.

4. Twins who grow up separately ...
   - **a.** always have different taste.
   - **b.** have different habits.
   - **c.** can never meet their soul mate.
   - **d.** might share similar habits.

UNIT 2

Coffee and Your Health

Have You Heard...?

People all around the world drink coffee, but not everyone drinks it the same way. Egyptians, for example, seldom add sugar, milk, or cream to their coffee — they like it black. Germans and the Swiss often fill half of their coffee cup with hot chocolate. People in Ethiopia drink their coffee with salt.

Before We Read

A. Read and Answer

Coffee is one of the most widely **consumed** drinks in the world. **Recent** studies show that coffee drinkers are less likely than nondrinkers to develop Alzheimer's, liver cancer, and diabetes. However, coffee isn't for everyone. Drinking coffee can **result in** sleep problems, **anxiety**, and faster **heart rates**. Too much **caffeine** might also increase the risk of **miscarriages** among **pregnant** women.

Write the words/phrases in bold above in the appropriate space. Change the form of the words if necessary.

	Word/Phrase	Definition
1		a substance in drinks that makes you more active
2		having a baby growing inside a woman's body
3		worry
4		to drink or eat something
5		to cause
6		a condition when a baby dies before it is born
7		having happened a short time ago
8		heartbeats per minute

TIP *The prefix **non–** means "not." So, **nondrinkers of coffee** refers to people who do not drink coffee.*

B. Make Predictions

Read the article on pages 22 and 23. Write the number of the paragraph to match each subtitle.

1. Importance of Right Amount of Coffee ______
2. Possible Negative Effects of Coffee ______
3. A Drink Loved by All ______
4. Coffee's Benefits ______

TIP *A **subtitle** helps readers understand the main idea in a paragraph.*

C. Scan

Read the article again. What are some of the benefits of drinking coffee?

- ☐ causes us to be energetic
- ☐ keeps us awake and aware
- ☐ makes us feel shaky
- ☐ makes it easier for us to sleep
- ☐ helps when we have stomachaches
- ☐ prevents some types of cancer

A Coffee a Day Keeps the Doctor Away

Track 03

If you look around, there are probably many coffeehouses near you. Coffee is big, big business. According to the Wall Street Journal, people around the world drink over 2 billion cups of coffee every day.

Although coffee is one of the world's most popular drinks, many people believe it isn't healthy. Coffee can make you feel more stress, and it can result in sleep problems and make you feel anxiety. Some people can't sleep all night if they drink coffee before bed. It has also been blamed for high heart rates, high blood pressure, and stomach problems.

One common belief is that some women who drink coffee may have a hard time becoming pregnant. Some researchers believe coffee can cause low birth weights or miscarriages when it is consumed by pregnant women.

Medical research, however, has started suggesting that coffee might actually be good for us. In addition to giving us energy and keeping us alert, coffee is thought to be helpful for headaches. As coffee also contains antioxidants,* it can protect our bodies against harmful substances in things like smoke and pollution.

Recent studies have found that coffee helps to prevent certain types of cancer. One study in Tokyo, for example, discovered that coffee drinkers were half as likely as nondrinkers to have liver cancer. Overall, the research shows that coffee is far more healthful than it is harmful.

While coffee may have health benefits, it is also full of caffeine which can make us feel excited and shaky.* However, **these problems** can be controlled by limiting the amount of coffee we drink. There is little evidence showing that coffee is truly harmful for normal people, and every day there is more evidence showing that it is good for us.

Reference:

* **antioxidants** *something you eat or drink that cleans your body*
* **shaky** *not firm; moving*

Comprehension Check

A. Short Answers

Write the answer.

1. Q: How much coffee is consumed every day?
   A: ______________________________

2. Q: What could happen if some people drink coffee before going to bed?
   A: ______________________________

3. Q: What type of cancer are coffee drinkers less likely to have than other people?
   A: ______________________________

4. Q: What is the overall finding of the research in Tokyo?
   A: ______________________________

5. Q: What substance in coffee can make us excited and shaky?
   A: ______________________________

B. True or False

*Check **True** or **False**.*

	True	False
1. The coffee industry doesn't make very much money.	☐	☐
2. Some researchers think coffee can lead to miscarriages.	☐	☐
3. Coffee gives people energy and keeps them awake.	☐	☐
4. Antioxidants contained in coffee are harmful to the human body.	☐	☐
5. Coffee drinkers are more likely to have liver cancer.	☐	☐
6. Coffee is high in caffeine.	☐	☐
7. Some bad effects of coffee can be solved by drinking less.	☐	☐
8. There is a lot of evidence that coffee hurts people's body.	☐	☐

C. Fill in the Blanks

Complete the sentences with the words from the article.

1. Many people ____________ coffee for high heart rates, high blood pressure, and breathing problems.
2. One common belief is that some women may have a hard time becoming ____________ when they drink coffee.
3. People think coffee not only gives us energy and keeps us alert but also works for ____________.
4. It is discovered that coffee drinkers were ____________ as likely as nondrinkers to have liver cancers.
5. In general, scientists say that coffee is much more ____________ than it is harmful.
6. Coffee is full of ____________ which can make us feel excited and shaky.

D. Vocabulary Building

Choose the synonym of the word/phrase in bold.

1. Jim is **having a hard time** finding a job.
   a. having trouble **b.** having luck with
2. I **consume** two glasses of milk per day.
   a. drink **b.** pour
3. The results of the test **suggest** that oranges are very healthy.
   a. feel **b.** indicate
4. **In addition to** being a good boss, Christine is a nice friend.
   a. except **b.** along with
5. A security guard must be **alert** at all times.
   a. aware **b.** tired
6. Tommy's parents **prevented** him from going out late at night.
   a. allowed **b.** stopped
7. Joe **discovered** a hot spring while hiking.
   a. left **b.** found
8. **Overall**, the team played well this season.
   a. at least **b.** generally
9. The police couldn't find any **evidence** that the man stole Diana's bag.
   a. story **b.** proof
10. The gift you sent was **truly** special.
   a. really **b.** mostly

E. Multiple Choice

Circle the answer.

1. What is the reading mainly about?
   a. coffee's effects on cancer
   b. Japanese people's views about coffee
   c. coffee's effects on health
   d. the reason why coffee is less popular

2. Some doctors say coffee ...
   a. can give us headaches.
   b. prevents all types of cancer.
   c. doesn't keep us awake.
   d. causes sleeplessness for some people.

3. Which of the following is NOT mentioned?
   a. Coffee is only grown in tropical areas.
   b. Drinking less coffee can control how shaky one gets.
   c. Coffeehouses are common everywhere.
   d. Some doctors believe coffee is unhealthy for pregnant women.

4. What does **these problems** refer to in the last paragraph?
   a. headaches and pregnancy problems
   b. feeling too active and shaky
   c. low blood pressure and heart rate
   d. not having energy and focus

5. Which of the following is true?
   a. Scientists say that drinking coffee can often help people sleep easily.
   b. A Japanese study says that coffee might cause several types of cancer.
   c. New research shows that coffee is probably more healthy than unhealthy.
   d. One organization says people begin drinking less coffee to be healthy.

Vocabulary Check

A. Meanings in Context

Choose the meaning of the sentence.

1. **According to** the police, the man was attacked on his way home last night.
   a. The man says the police told him last night that he would be attacked.
   b. The police say the man was attacked on his way home last night.

2. With all the noise, Janice **had a hard time** falling asleep.
   a. It was difficult for Janice to fall asleep because of the noise.
   b. The noise caused Janice to wake up early in the morning.

3. **In addition to** France, I would like to visit Germany and Spain.
   a. I want to visit France, Germany, and Spain.
   b. Germany and Spain are the only two countries I want to visit.

4. The room **is full of** old books and clothes.
   a. There is enough space to put more books and clothes there.
   b. There are a lot of old books and clothes in the room.

B. Complete the Sentences

Fill in the blanks with the words in the box. Change the form of the words if necessary.

evidence	substance	half	blame	alert	medical

1. Fatty food has been ____________ for causing heart problems.
2. It's expensive to receive ____________ care in the U.S.
3. Dave says he isn't ____________ in the morning until he has had breakfast.
4. The woman looked in her cup and saw a dark ____________ in her tea.
5. Baltimore has ____________ the amount of people that San Diego has.
6. There is strong ____________ that these chemicals are bad for the environment.

C. Words with Different Meanings

Match the word in bold with its definition.

1 The nurse just took my blood **pressure**. ______
Exercise is a good way to relieve **pressure**. ______
Definition: ⓐ *n.* a force against another thing ⓑ *n.* anxiety

2 **Stress** can cause a lot of health problems. ______
Japanese people put **stress** on politeness. ______
Definition: ⓐ *n.* special attention ⓑ *n.* worry

3 Maria stayed **up** all night to prepare for the exam. ______
Put your hand **up** if you know the answer. ______
Definition: ⓐ *prep.* to a higher place ⓑ *prep.* not in bed

4 The research **suggests** that only 15 percent of the population trusts the government. ______
I **suggested** that Joan ask her father for his opinion. ______
Definition: ⓐ *v.* to show ⓑ *v.* to tell people what they should do

Reading Strategy

Understanding Cause and Effect

TIP

A cause explains why something happens, while an effect shows what happens. Here are some common words for expressing cause and effect.

because	since	as	therefore
so	as a result	because of	due to
cause	be blamed for	result in	for this reason

• Give It a Try •

PART I

*Write **a** or **b** in the blank.*

1. It is believed that ______________ can **result in** ______________.
   a. heart and stomach problems   b. coffee
2. Problems **caused by** ______________ include ______________.
   a. stress and sleep difficulties   b. coffee
3. Some experts **blame** ______________ **for** ______________.
   a. caffeine   b. miscarriages in pregnant women
4. **Since** ______________, ______________.
   a. it protects us from harmful substances   b. coffee is rich in antioxidants
5. ______________ **because** ______________.
   a. I feel shaky and anxious   b. I consume too much caffeine

PART II

Complete the passage with the words in the box. Change the form of the words if necessary.

due to	result	so	cause

My father made a big change in his life. He used to smoke cigarettes all the time. But then one day, he realized that he couldn't climb the stairs to his apartment without stopping to cough. This **1.** ______________ him to quit smoking cigarettes. **2.** ______________ this decision, his health improved greatly. He noticed that he was feeling more and more energetic, **3.** ______________ he made some more changes. He stopped drinking soda and eating unhealthy foods. His new lifestyle **4.** ______________ in a greater love for exercise. He now runs three times a week and often plays basketball on the weekends with people half his age.

Further Reading

The Legend of Coffee

Track 04

One of the most famous legends of the discovery of coffee is "The Story of the Shepherd.*" A long time ago, there was an Ethiopian shepherd named Kaldi. One day, his sheep couldn't stop running around. Kaldi was very curious about this. He started watching them carefully. Eventually, he found the sheep eating red fruit that looked like cherries. He decided to try **some** too and soon felt excited and full of energy. He shared the fruit with monks from the area, and their reaction was the same. Today, many people believe that they were eating coffee beans.

The history of coffee goes back to the 15th century. It is thought that Ethiopians were the first to discover the coffee plant. From there, coffee spread to Egypt and Yemen. Coffee beans were first roasted and brewed* in Arabia. By the 16th century, they had reached all of Africa and the Middle East. Coffee arrived in Istanbul in 1543, and the drink became a big part of the city's culture. People would go to coffeehouses to discuss literature and play chess. Coffee then reached Europe through the ports of Venice. Coffeehouses became popular among writers, artists, and philosophers in Paris and London. The British began calling them penny universities because it cost a penny to enter and chat with the intellectuals inside. The popular drink was later introduced to Indonesia and the Americas.

Today, coffee is the second most popular drink in the world after water. In fact, people love coffee so much that it has its own holidays. In Ireland, Coffee Day is on September 19th; in Japan, people celebrate on October 1st. South Americans especially love coffee. In 2001, Brazil sold a stamp that smelled like Brazilian coffee! All around the world, people love waking up to the smell of fresh coffee.

Reference:

* **shepherd** *someone who takes care of sheep as a job*

* **brew** *to make a drink of coffee or tea*

Comprehension Check

A. Put in Order

Put the following events in order.

a. Coffee was brought to Indonesia and the Americas.
b. People in England started calling coffeehouses penny universities.
c. Coffee became a big part of the culture of Istanbul.
d. Ethiopians probably discovered the coffee plant first.
e. The people of Venice began drinking coffee.
f. Arabia was the first place that coffee beans were roasted and brewed.

_____ → _____ → _____ → _____ → _____ → _____

B. Complete the Passage

Fill in the blanks with the words in the box.

educated	daily	spread	shepherd	behind

Experts say that coffee was discovered by Ethiopians in the 1400s. According to one story, an Ethiopian **1.** ____________ noticed that his sheep became very energetic after eating a type of red fruit from a tree. After that, coffee beans started to **2.** ____________ all over the world. Coffee became a big part of the culture of many countries, starting in Africa, the Middle East, and Europe. Coffeehouses became very popular among **3.** ____________ people such as writers and philosophers. In modern times, coffee has become the No. 2 drink in the world **4.** ____________ water. Ireland and Japan have their own coffee holidays. Brazil has even sold a stamp that smells like coffee. People around the world really love their **5.** ____________ cup of coffee.

C. Multiple Choice

Circle the answer.

1. What is the reading mainly about?
a. a story about a shepherd
b. the history of coffee
c. special coffee days
d. coffeehouses in Europe

2. What does **some** refer to in the first paragraph?
a. red fruit
b. coffeehouses
c. cherries
d. sheep

3. Why did the British call coffeehouses penny universities?
a. Only university students could enter the coffeehouses.
b. Students took classes in coffeehouses.
c. Some universities brewed coffee.
d. People could spend time at coffeehouses when they paid a penny for coffee.

UNIT 3 Basketball Fever

Have You Heard...?

People have been watching LeBron James since he was a high school freshman in Akron, Ohio. During his first season, James scored 21 points a game, leading his team to the state championship. Over four years, James' team, the Fighting Irish, lost only six times. *More than a Game*, a documentary, tells the story of this team's success from the start.

Before We Read

A. Make Predictions

Read the last sentence on page 33. What do you think the reading is about?

- ☐ the history of the YMCA
- ☐ how basketball has changed through the ages
- ☐ how the game has become international
- ☐ the reasons basketball is the greatest sport

TIP *The writer often emphasizes the main idea again in the last sentence, called the* ***conclusion****.*

B. Read and Answer

Read the article on pages 32 and 33. Fill in the blanks with the words in the box. Change the form of the words if necessary.

Olympic	peach	legal	win	invent

All About Basketball

- James Naismith, a teacher at a YMCA in Massachusetts, is **credited** with ____________ basketball.
- The first **hoops** were actually ____________ baskets, and **backboards** were made of wire.
- The sport became a(n) ____________ event at the Berlin Summer Games in 1936.
- In 1967, it was illegal to **slam-dunk**. Nine years later, it was ____________ again.
- Michael Jordan is a **legend** in the world of basketball. During his career, the Chicago Bulls ____________ six NBA **championships**.

Write the words in bold above in the appropriate space. Change the form of the words if necessary.

	Word	Definition
1		someone who is greatly admired
2		to believe someone has done something good
3		contents for the top position
4		the board behind the basket
5		the ring that you throw the ball through
6		to push a ball down through the basket

C. Scan

Read the article again. What do the following numbers refer to?

a. the time the color of the ball was changed
b. how many years it took to invent a basketball
c. the year hoops were introduced
d. the year Naismith had a great idea

1. 1891 ______ **2.** 1913 ______ **3.** 40 ______ **4.** 1950s ______

Basketball's Rise to Popularity

Track 05

James Harden makes a perfect pass. DeAndre Jordon flies through the air and slam-dunks. Russell Westbrook steals the ball and runs down the court. This is the NBA, and fans around the world are crazy about it. Most of this league's teams are from America, but the big-money* game of basketball owes everything to a man from Canada — Dr. James Naismith.

In 1891, Naismith was teaching at the YMCA International Training School on America's northeast coast. Long, cold winters there made exercise difficult. When trying to think of a winter game for his students, this clever Canadian had a lightbulb moment. Borrowing from a game he had played as a child, Naismith invented a sport his students could play indoors. He put two peach baskets on the walls at either end of a court. The players had to run and throw the ball into the baskets. That's how basketball was born.

Basketball caught on in the U.S., and the game changed a lot. The first games at the YMCA didn't have dribbling. In 1913, the peach baskets were replaced by metal hoops with nets. Before that time, players had to use a broomstick* to get the ball out of the basket every time someone scored. Another change was the creation of the backboard. In the beginning, players could use the walls of the gym to score a basket. A few years later, the backboard was extended 60 centimeters from the wall.

The first time Naismith's students played basketball, they used a soccer ball. It took almost 40 years for a basketball to be created. The orange basketball we know today wasn't invented until the late 1950s. Previously, basketballs were brown. Ever since its invention, basketball has grown in popularity. In 1936 — three years before Naismith's death — the game even became an Olympic sport. From small beginnings at a YMCA in Springfield, Massachusetts, the game has now spread around the world.

Reference:

* **big-money** *involving a lot of money*
* **broomstick** *the long handle of a broom*

NBA Fun Facts

At 231 centimeters, Gheorghe Muresan was the NBA's tallest player. His hands were 30 centimeters. Another big man, Shaquille O'Neal, had a shoe size of 22, about 400mm. Besides winning championships, O'Neal will be remembered for his strength. At one time, he could pull a whole backboard down by himself.

Comprehension Check

A. Fill in the Blanks

Complete the sentences with the words from the article. Change the form of the words if necessary.

1. The big-money game of basketball ______________ everything to the man who invented it.
2. When Dr. James Naismith created basketball, he ______________ ideas from a game he had played as a child.
3. At first, basketball didn't have ______________. Players either ran with the ball or passed it.
4. Basketball players threw the ball into peach baskets until the baskets were ______________ by metal hoops with ______________ in 1913.
5. The backboard was ______________ 60 centimeters out from the wall after a few years later of creation.
6. Basketballs are now orange. ______________, they were brown.
7. Basketball's ______________ has grown ever since it was invented.
8. Invented in Springfield, Massachusetts, basketball has now ______________ to most countries in the world.

B. Put in Order

Put the following events in order.

a. Dr. Naismith came up with a game that could be played inside.
b. Basketball became an Olympic sport almost 80 years ago.
c. Dr. Naismith moved to America to teach.
d. Players didn't bounce the ball at first.
e. A new, orange ball was introduced to the game.
f. The backboard was moved away from the wall.
g. They decided to stop using peach baskets.
h. Dr. Naismith reminded that he played a game like basketball when he was a child.

_____ → _____ → _____ → _____ → _____ → _____ → _____ → _____

C. True or False

*Check **True** or **False**.*

		True	False
1.	Basketball is America's traditional sport for centuries.	☐	☐
2.	The game was invented in the 18th century.	☐	☐
3.	At first, players threw the ball into a peach basket.	☐	☐
4.	Players have always dribbled the ball at first.	☐	☐
5.	Dr. Naismith invented the game of basketball for his son.	☐	☐
6.	Basketball became an Olympic sport in 1913.	☐	☐
7.	Players used a broomstick to get the ball out of the basket in its early years.	☐	☐
8.	At one time, basketballs were brown, not orange.	☐	☐

D. Vocabulary Building

Circle the synonym of the word/phrase in bold.

1. This bag is **perfect** for me.
   a. boring b. ideal
2. Dolphins are **clever**. We can teach them to do lots of tricks.
   a. intelligent b. emotional
3. The telephone was **invented** by Alexander Graham Bell in 1876.
   a. created b. found
4. You can get bubble tea in San Francisco, but it never really **caught on** in America.
   a. was discovered b. became popular
5. Pavel has lived in London for four years. **Previously**, he lived in Moscow.
   a. While b. Before
6. Mariah Carey's **popularity** has declined over the past ten years.
   a. fame b. similarity

Circle the antonym of the word/phrase in bold.

1. Russel **stole** the ball from the player on the Bulls before he could pass it.
   a. gave b. got
2. Carrie is **crazy about** photography. She takes her camera everywhere she goes.
   a. tired of b. interested in
3. We have to stay **indoors** today because it's raining.
   a. inside b. outside
4. Eric **dribbled** the ball around two players and then took a shot.
   a. held b. jumped
5. Ivan **scored** three times in the hockey game tonight.
   a. gain b. missed
6. After Mr. Kesler's **death**, his son took over the company.
   a. passing away b. birth

E. Multiple Choice

Circle the answer.

1. Most of the NBA league's teams are found in ...
   a. Canada.
   b. the States.
   c. Massachusetts.
   d. the Olympics.

2. What did Dr. Naismith do?
   a. He educated students.
   b. He worked for the NBA.
   c. He built gyms for people.
   d. He owned the YMCA.

3. Why did Dr. Naismith invent basketball?
   a. He was hoping to become rich.
   b. He was looking for an indoor sport.
   c. His students got bored with soccer.
   d. He had too many peach baskets.

4. How has the game changed?
   a. Players now use a ball to play.
   b. We have a new name for the game.
   c. It's not allowed to slam-dunk.
   d. Players don't need a stick anymore.

Vocabulary Check

A. Topic Words

Use the topic words in the box to complete the sentences. Change the form of the words if necessary.

pass	steal	court	dribble	score

1. When a player makes a ____________, he or she throws the ball to a teammate.
2. A ____________ is an area made for certain sports, such as basketball or tennis.
3. When we take the ball from a player on the other team, we are ____________ it.
4. Throwing the ball through the basket is called ____________ a basket.
5. Basketball players cannot run without ____________ the ball for more than one and a half steps.

B. Fill in the Missing Letters

Complete the sentences with the words from the article.

1. My brother is a big **f**____________ of Elvis Presley.
   (a person who likes something or someone very much)
2. In his first year in the **l**____________, Gretzky scored 137 points.
   (a group of teams that play each other)
3. Many English words, like ballet, are **b**____________ from French.
   (use a word from another language)
4. We shouldn't stay **i**____________ on such a sunny day. Let's go outside!
   (inside)
5. They **r**____________ all the carpets before moving in.
   (use something else)
6. The habit of tea drinking was **s**____________ to Japan from China.
   (extend over an area)

C. Meanings in Context

Choose the meaning of the sentence.

1. Jeffrey **is crazy about** model airplanes.
   a. Jeffrey is not interested in model airplanes.
   b. Jeffrey likes model airplanes very much.

2. I passed the English test. I **owe** it all **to** my tutor.
   a. My tutor cost me a lot of money.
   b. My tutor helped me pass the English test.

3. When the apple fell on Isaac Newton's head, he **had a lightbulb moment** about gravity.
   a. He suddenly understood something very clearly.
   b. He couldn't understand the idea at all.

4. Baseball first **caught on** in the south of Taiwan. Then it spread north.
   a. People all over Taiwan have always loved watching baseball.
   b. People in the south part of Taiwan first started to watch and enjoy baseball.

Reading Strategy

Understanding Time Order

TIP

Writers often need to tell things in order. When doing so, dates are useful. For example, the year, month, week, day, or hour can explain something more clearly. Other clue words include:

first	then	since	when	previously
while	immediately	before	shortly	after
next	for	by the time	in the beginning	until

• Give It a Try •

PART I

Choose the sentence that is written in time order. Underline the clue words.

1. **a.** At first, Abraham Lincoln was a lawyer. Then in 1860 he became president.
b. Abraham Lincoln was over 180 centimeters tall. And he had a dark beard.

2. **a.** I've never been to Egypt. I've heard that people don't normally go there in summer. Sometimes, the temperature is over 45 degrees Celsius.
b. After my bags had passed through airport security, I walked to gate four. 30 minutes later, I was getting on a plane to Egypt.

PART II

Choose the answer.

Steve Nash of the Phoenix Suns was one of the best basketball players in the world. But **1.** ______________, he didn't get much respect in the NBA. Nash didn't go to a well-known college, so people didn't know who he was. He only played about ten minutes per game in his **2.** ______________ NBA season. During his second year, he started to play a lot more. It wasn't **3.** ______________ the 2000-01 season that Nash really started playing well. **4.** ______________ he won his second MVP award, every basketball fan knew his name.

1. **a.** beginner	**b.** their beginning	**c.** in the beginning	**d.** a beginning time of
2. **a.** number one	**b.** first	**c.** at first	**d.** firstly
3. **a.** while	**b.** after	**c.** before	**d.** until
4. **a.** By the time	**b.** Next	**c.** Immediately	**d.** Then

Further Reading

The King Has Arrived

Track 06

Running down the court like a speeding train, LeBron James comes up from behind the other team's player and blocks **his** shot. Plays like this show why King James is one of the most exciting players in the NBA.

James was the first choice in the 2003 NBA Draft* at age 18. Since then, he has entertained fans on and off the court. In his first season, he won the Rookie* of the Year after scoring more than 20 points per game. Three years later, the Cleveland Cavaliers played in their first finals. James **took home** the league's Most Valuable Player award four times. James also has shown the ability to make people laugh while acting in funny commercials and hosting a TV show. Because of his performance skills and personality, companies pay James more than $28 million each year to be a symbol for their products.

James is one of only three NBA players in history to score 30 points, give out seven assists,* and take down seven rebounds* per game in a full season. Superstars Michael Jordan and Oscar Robertson are the other two. James has scored a lot of points and made a lot of money, but there was one larger goal that he aimed to achieve: an NBA championship. "It's one of the ultimate goals for me as a basketball player," James said on a television news show. With his talent and desire, James led the Miami Heat to win two championships. Now the only question remaining is how many he'll have by the time his career is over.

Player Info

Photo: Keith Allison

Full Name: LeBron Raymone James
Nickname: King James
Birthday: December 30th, 1984
Birthplace: Akron, Ohio
Height: 203 cm
Weight: 113 kg
NBA Career: Since 2003
Fun Facts:

- has the same birthday as Tiger Woods, who is nine years older
- eats and writes with his left hand, but shoots the ball with his right hand
- a good friend of rapper Jay-Z

Reference:

* **draft** *when teams choose players to join them*
* **assist** *giving the ball to a player who scores*
* **rookie** *someone who's just started playing*
* **rebound** *catching a ball after a player misses a shot*

Comprehension Check

A. Fill in the Blanks

Complete the sentences with the words from the article.

1. 2003: LeBron James was selected first in the NBA ____________ by the Cleveland Cavaliers.
2. 2004: LeBron James was named NBA ____________ of the Year in his first season.
3. 2007: The Cleveland Cavaliers played in the NBA ____________ for the first time.
4. since 2006: LeBron James wins NBA Most ____________ Player.

B. Summary

Choose the answer.

LeBron James, one of the most exciting players in basketball, was chosen **1.** ____________ in the 2003 NBA Draft at age 18. After scoring around 20 points a game in his first season, James was **2.** ____________ Rookie of the Year. Over the years, LeBron has improved a lot. In one season, he even **3.** ____________ 30 points, made seven assists, and got seven **4.** ____________ per game. Although James' team made it to the finals in 2007, they didn't win the championship. According to James, this was his **5.** ____________ goal. He has accomplished this goal twice so far.

1. **a.** the first	**b.** firstly	**c.** first	**d.** in first
2. **a.** dropped	**b.** expelled	**c.** dismissed	**d.** named
3. **a.** score	**b.** scoring	**c.** scored	**d.** had scored
4. **a.** baskets	**b.** dollars	**c.** rebounds	**d.** passes
5. **a.** ultimate	**b.** nearest	**c.** important	**d.** helpful

C. Multiple Choice

Circle the answer.

1. What is the reading mainly about?
   a. to introduce the achievements of LeBron James
   b. to talk more about the history of the Cavaliers
   c. to explain who Jordan and Robertson are
   d. to let readers know James was chosen in 2003 in the NBA Draft

2. What does **his** refer to in the first paragraph?
   a. LeBron James
   b. another player on the opposing team
   c. the NBA
   d. the most exciting player

3. What does **took home** mean in the context of the second paragraph?
   a. won
   b. lost
   c. got points
   d. named Rookie of the Year

4. How does the writer describe LeBron James?
   a. as a very large player
   b. as someone who likes trains
   c. as being talented on and off the court
   d. as a person only girls desire

UNIT 4

Caring for the Environment

Have You Heard...?

While it started in the United States over 40 years ago, Earth Day has truly gone international. Every year on the first day of spring, over 90 percent of the world's countries take part in Earth Day. In fact, it's the largest celebration in the world that is not religious. Earth Day has its own website, blog, logo, flag, and even a TV station, called Earth Day TV.

Before We Read

A. Read and Answer

In 2015, people all over the world **celebrated** the 45th birthday of Earth Day. During the celebration, people were **encouraged** to improve their green practices and have **earth-friendly** habits, such as taking **public transportation**. For the 45th birthday, environmental **organizations** asked people to think about **global** warming too. What can you do about it? Pick up garbage in the street or try walking as much as possible. And don't forget the three Rs of protecting life everywhere: **Reduce**, Reuse, and **Recycle**.

Write the words/phrases in bold above in the appropriate space. Change the form of the words if necessary.

	Word/Phrase	Definition
1		to process something in order to use it again
2		buses, trains, or the subway
3		to try to talk someone into doing something
4		to make something less or smaller
5		a group
6		relating to the whole world
7		to do something special to mark an event
8		not damaging the environment

B. Make Predictions

Look at the pictures and the captions on pages 42 and 43. Answer the questions.

1. What is the main idea of the reading?
   - ☐ Children need to read books about Earth Day.
   - ☐ There are many different ways for people to get involved on Earth Day.
   - ☐ It is difficult for children to do something on Earth Day.
   - ☐ Dirty streets need to be cleaned up on Earth Day.

TIP
We can predict the main idea of an article by looking at pictures. They often come with an explanation below them, called a ***caption****.*

2. What is one topic that we can find in the article?
   - ☐ how to reduce waste
   - ☐ drinking two bottles of water a day
   - ☐ siblings working together for community
   - ☐ people holding up signs

Earth Day Every Day

Track 07

Earth Day, which falls on April 22nd, is the day to clean up our environment.

On April 22nd, people around the world celebrate something they all have in common — the earth. Earth Day is a celebration that began in America in 1970. On that day, a U.S. politician called on the country's people to protest against environmental pollution which leads to global warming. Tens of millions of Americans took to the streets for a peaceful demonstration. Earth Day is now celebrated by over a billion people in around 180 countries.

Save energy by turning off the lights.

What do people do on this day? At first, people simply listened to speeches. These days, there are parades and information fairs, where you can learn about environmental problems and solutions. Many schools have students make posters. The posters encourage green practices, like recycling and taking public transportation. Some people choose to plant trees or pick up trash in parks and natural areas. Environmental organizations use Earth Day to inform the public of the damage which people do to the earth. Once more people know the problems, everyone can take more steps to solve them.

Reuse water bottles to save money and help the earth.

To do your part in protecting life on earth, follow three simple rules: Reduce, Reuse, and Recycle. First, reduce the amount of energy you use and the waste you produce. Turn the lights and TV off when you leave the room. This will cut down on the amount of electricity you use. Try to use dishes that can be reused when you eat at a restaurant or at home. You can also reduce waste by not eating takeout.* When you get takeout, you get a lot of extra paper and plastic.

Next, try to reuse what you buy. Don't purchase a new bottle of water every time you're thirsty. Instead, refill bottles at home. Paper is another item you can reuse. Did you know that it takes 24 trees to make a ton* of paper? By cutting out the unused areas of paper, you can save trees.

Finally, if you can't reuse something, don't throw it away. Recycle it! It may take a little time to sort through the trash, but the earth will thank you.

You don't have to wait until April 22nd to start your earth-friendly habits. Go outside today, and think about ways you can make every day Earth Day.

Reference:

* **takeout** *a meal that you buy at a restaurant to eat at home*
* **ton** *a unit of weight (one metric ton = 1,000 kilograms)*

Comprehension Check

A. Main Idea

Write the number of the paragraph to match each topic.

1. popular Earth Day activities ______
2. using things more than once ______
3. the origin of Earth Day ______
4. making everyday Earth Day ______
5. trying to waste less ______
6. not throwing away everything ______

B. True or False

*Check **True** or **False**.*

	True	False
1. People use Earth Day to inform the public of our environmental problems.	☐	☐
2. Many Earth Day posters warn people about a demonstration.	☐	☐
3. On the first Earth Day, people held many activities to celebrate it.	☐	☐
4. Eating takeout will help reduce waste.	☐	☐
5. You should try to reuse what you buy.	☐	☐
6. Turning off the lights when you don't need them saves energy.	☐	☐
7. If something can't be reused, you should throw it away immediately.	☐	☐
8. Use both sides of paper will help save trees and our earth.	☐	☐

C. Topic Words

Write the type of the rule to match each statement.

a. reduce	**b.** reuse	**c.** recycle

1. Give away old clothes to someone who needs them. ______
2. Use public transportation. ______
3. Sort garbage into paper, plastic, and metal before throwing it away. ______
4. Call the city government to collect old furniture. ______
5. Turn off the computer when it's not in use. ______
6. Use energy-saving bulbs instead of traditional ones. ______
7. Carry your own shopping bags. ______
8. Put flowers in an old water bottle. ______

D. Vocabulary Building

Circle the synonym of the word in bold.

1. Scientists say the **earth** is home to about 10,000 types of birds.
   a. energy   b. planet
2. The **demonstration** became dangerous, so the police were called.
   a. treatment   b. protest
3. By 1990, over 200 million people in 141 **countries** were celebrating Earth Day.
   a. nations   b. provinces
4. To cancel your credit card, **simply** call this number.
   a. just   b. then
5. The worker at the sandwich shop gives me **extra** sauce if I ask for it.
   a. additional   b. strong
6. Try not to **purchase** products that use a lot of packaging.
   a. wrap   b. buy
7. Don't throw away an old **item**. If it is broken, you can repair it.
   a. waste   b. thing
8. We can prevent pollution by using **green** cleaning products.
   a. dangerous   b. earth-friendly

Circle the antonym of the word in bold.

1. A **peaceful** demonstration was held for environmental issues.
   a. violent   b. relaxed
2. Students are **encouraged** to take part in the event.
   a. helped   b. prevented
3. We should do more to **protect** the environment.
   a. save   b. damage
4. The doctor told the patient to **reduce** the amount of salt in his diet.
   a. keep   b. increase

E. Multiple Choice

Circle the answer.

1. On the first Earth Day, people ...
   a. watched to the news.
   b. enjoyed nature.
   c. heard speeches.
   d. took the class.

2. Why do students make posters?
   a. to get more people to cut down trees
   b. to encourage people to care about the environment
   c. to win a contest for the best poster
   d. to raise lots of money for Earth Day

3. Turning off unnecessary lights will help cut down on the amount of ...
   a. paper.   b. electricity.
   c. water.   d. plastic.

4. If we use things that can be washed and used again, which rule are we following?
   a. reuse   b. recycle
   c. reduce   d. rebuild

5. Which of the following is NOT a solution to environmental problems?
   a. planting trees   b. reusing bottles
   c. purchasing cars   d. using public transportation

Vocabulary Check

A. Complete the Sentences

Fill in the blanks with the words in the box. Change the form of the words if necessary.

protest	damage	waste

1. Luckily, the earthquake didn't cause any serious ____________.
2. Three people got hurt in the ____________ yesterday.
3. The house had been badly ____________ by fire.
4. It's important to recycle household ____________.
5. Hundreds of people were ____________ outside the mayor's office.
6. Leaving the computer on all the time ____________ energy.

B. Words with Different Meanings

Match the word in bold with its definition.

1. Our boss has tried to be **fair** to all the workers. _____
   After Alex finished school, he went to a job **fair** to find some work. _____
   Definition: ⓐ *n.* an event where people get information or buy things ⓑ *adj.* treating people right

2. James likes to take **public** transportation, like a bus or a subway. _____
   This meeting will be open to the **public**. _____
   Definition: ⓐ *n.* ordinary people ⓑ *adj.* for everyone to use

3. He said that global warming could be the end of **life** on earth. _____
   The family moved to the country to start a new, quiet **life**. _____
   Definition: ⓐ *n.* living things ⓑ *n.* a lifestyle

4. Could you please wash the **dishes**? _____
   This **dish** is best served hot. _____
   Definition: ⓐ *n.* a plate or bowl ⓑ *n.* food cooked in a particular way

5. I **sorted** my old clothes into piles and sent them to people who needed them. _____
   Eddie likes all **sorts** of food. He's not picky. _____
   Definition: ⓐ *n.* a type or kind ⓑ *v.* to arrange things in groups

C. Word Definitions

Match the word with its definition.

organization •	• a talk in front of people
peaceful •	• a public celebration
demonstration •	• one kind of power
speech •	• an official group of people
parade •	• an event in which people meet to protest or support something
electricity •	• no fighting; quiet and calm

Reading Strategy

The Order of Events: Listing / Processes

TIP

We use sequence words or phrases to show the order in which things happen. Here are some common words and phrases for expressing the order of events.

first	then	later on	third
first of all	second	next	afterwards
to begin with	the next step	at the same time	finally/lastly

• Give It a Try •

PART I

Complete the passage with the words in the box.

next	later	second	finally	to begin with

How to Plant a Tree for Earth Day

1. ______________, choose a tree that can survive in the weather of your area. **2.** ______________, find an area where your tree can grow. **3.** ______________, ask your family and friends to help you plant your tree. This will help more people learn about helping the earth. **4.** ______________ on, create a schedule to remind yourself to maintain the tree. **5.** ______________, don't stop there! Think of other places to plant trees in your town.

PART II

Put the following events in order.

Pumpkin Pie Recipe

a. Lastly, cool the pie and serve it to friends.
b. First, set the temperature at 190 degrees Celsius.
c. Afterwards, pour the pumpkin mixture into the pie crust and bake 35 to 40 minutes.
d. The next step is to add two cups of cooked pumpkin, two cups of milk, a half cup of brown sugar, and a half teaspoon of salt.
e. At the same time, mix everything with the eggs.
f. Second, mix two eggs in a bowl.

_____ → _____ → _____ → _____ → _____ → _____

Further Reading

The Emerald* City Goes Green

Track 08

Seattle is located in Washington, between three national parks. From early on, many local businesses were logging companies that did work in the harbor. Now, after almost 200 years of development, the city's government and residents have returned to nature.

Seattle started out as a logging town in the mid-1800s. The arrival of Microsoft more than a century later helped Seattle become known as an important city for technology. The coffee shop Starbucks helped the city become known for its great coffee too. Not long after, Seattle started recycling and quickly became one of the greenest cities in America.

Seattle has long been seen as a place that uses a green city design. In 1999, for example, the city began the Street Edge Alternative* (SEA) Streets Project. This project lined city streets with plants. Residents are now happily parking their cars next to flower gardens and trees.

The Green Up Program is an effort to create power in Seattle in a green way. Residents can choose to buy it from wind farms and other renewable* energy sources. Green power is more expensive, but it is keeping Seattle cleaner.

Residents are also being encouraged to drive their cars less. As part of the One Less Car Challenge, families give up driving one of their cars. In return, they receive discounts on earth-friendly products and coupons* for public transportation.

Green buildings are another trend in Seattle. The Ballard Library is a good example. Its roof is covered with plants that collect rainwater. Natural light shines through the windows. Visitors like the space for its earth-friendliness and beauty. The look of Seattle has changed over the years. Many of the city's residents now see it is possible to live in harmony with their environment. Perhaps one day Seattle will be just like the natural areas outside of the city.

Seattle Quick Facts

Country: United States
State: Washington
Population: 650,000 (25th largest in the U.S.)
Nickname: The Emerald City
Cloudy Days per Year: 226
Famous Landmarks:
the Space Needle, the first Starbucks, Bill Gates' house, Pike Place Fish Market
Known for:
coffee, rock music, rain, city parks, technology companies

Reference:

* **emerald** *green*
* **alternative** *offering a choice*
* **renewable** *able to replace itself naturally*
* **coupon** *a piece of paper that can get you a cheaper price*

Comprehension Check

A. Classification

Match the sentence with the type of program.

a. Street Edge Alternative (SEA)	**b.** Green Up	**c.** One Less Car Challenge

1. grow flowers along the sidewalk _____
2. take out your old bike and ride it to the office _____
3. get a ride from your friends instead of driving _____
4. plant a tree outside a Metro Transit station _____
5. use green power to keep Seattle cleaner _____

B. Fill in the Missing Letters

Complete the sentences with the words from the article.

1. People living in Seattle are trying to return to **n**__________ now.
2. Drivers are encouraged to take **p**__________ **t**__________ instead of their own cars.
3. Seattle lined city streets with **p**__________ so that people can see flower gardens and trees everywhere.
4. If you live in Seattle, people can get **p**__________ from wind farms.
5. A green building has a roof which is covered with plants that collect **r**__________.
6. Residents in Seattle can live with their **e**__________ in harmony.

C. Multiple Choice

Circle the answer.

1. When Seattle was founded, what was its main industry?
   - **a.** cutting down trees to sell the wood
   - **b.** building cars that used less gas
   - **c.** selling renewable energy sources
   - **d.** making computers and software

2. Seattle is probably best known for ...
   - **a.** traffic and lots of police.
   - **b.** mountains and winter sports.
   - **c.** technology companies and coffee.
   - **d.** sunlight and beaches.

3. What is true about Seattle?
   - **a.** Seattle is one of the most expensive American cities to live in.
   - **b.** The people in Seattle work with the government to make the city greener.
   - **c.** Seattle is one of the most popular places to buy flowers in America.
   - **d.** All of the technology companies in Seattle are now going green.

4. Which of the following is NOT mentioned in the article?
   - **a.** Seattle is now one of the greenest cities in America.
   - **b.** There are green programs to help the environment in Seattle.
   - **c.** One program in Seattle now asks people to drive less.
   - **d.** Many libraries have been built in Seattle.

UNIT 5

Table Manners

Have You Heard...?

Nobody is sure when we started using chopsticks, but there are stories of them going back 3,000 years. At first, chopsticks weren't the same size. They were used to take food out of pots, but not for eating. We used to call them *zhu* sticks, but sailors felt it was bad luck as *zhu* sounded like stop in Chinese. They wanted their ships to go fast, so the name was changed to *kuaizi*, fast sticks.

Before We Read

A. Read and Answer

Tips on Table Manners

- In Norway, Malaysia, and Germany, it is **rude** to leave food on your plate.
- In Egypt and Russia, it is considered an **insult** if you eat the complete meal. This shows that the host hasn't provided enough food.
- In Turkey, it's a **compliment** if you ask for more food.
- In Japan, the **guest of honor** sits at the center of the table, farthest from the door, and starts eating first.
- In the Middle East, leave food on your plate when you're finished, or it will be filled again.

Write the words/phrases in bold above in the appropriate space. Change the form of the words if necessary.

	Word/Phrase	Definition
1		what you say to show you admire something
2		impolite
3		the most important guest
4		the way how someone eats their food
5		something you do or say that shows disrespect
6		advice

B. Make Predictions

Read the first paragraph and the subtitles on pages 52 and 53. Answer the questions.

1. What do you think the reading is about?
   - ☐ the best dishes in the world
   - ☐ different customs for eating
   - ☐ how people eat noodles
   - ☐ following what others do

TIP

*Writers use **subtitles** when they want to change the subject. By looking at the subtitles, readers can understand the direction of the article.*

2. What manners will you probably learn from the reading? Choose three.
   - ☐ where to sit at the table
   - ☐ what to eat in Africa
   - ☐ who eats first in Europe
   - ☐ how loud to burp
   - ☐ how quiet to be during the meal
   - ☐ which fork to use while eating

Eating Your Way Around the World

Track 09

One way to make a good impression on people is to have nice table manners. Some manners are the same everywhere, like chewing with a closed mouth and thanking the host. But some countries can have very different ideas about what is considered polite.

Where to Sit?

In many Asian cultures, the seating arrangement is strict. The most important person sits in a central seat facing the door. The next most important person sits beside him or her, and so on. Guests must wait to be told where to sit. By contrast, where guests sit in the West often doesn't matter. Either the host or the guest of honor sits at the head of the table. However, it is polite to ask, "where should I sit?"

What to Do?

At a table in Europe, there may be several forks, knives, and spoons. It is proper to start with the tableware* farthest from the plate and use a new utensil* for each part of the meal. In the Middle East and parts of Africa, however, everyone eats with their fingers, but only with the right hand. People in some parts of Africa also don't show the bottom of their feet if they're eating on a carpet. In Japan and China, people lift a bowl of rice to their mouth and eat with chopsticks. Koreans, on the other hand, think it's rude to pick up their rice bowl. They eat their rice with a spoon.

How Quiet to Be?

In the West, making noise while eating soup is rude and may cause others to stare at you. In Japan, however, loudly slurping* soup and ramen is the polite, correct way to eat. Burping* and chewing loudly are also impolite in America and Europe, but in China, **those habits** are fine. They show enjoyment of the meal.

If you're not sure how to act, it's best to follow what other people are doing. As long as you show respect, most people will forgive you for breaking minor rules.

Reference:

* **tableware** *knives, spoons, and forks*
* **utensil** *a tool used in a household, especially a kitchen*
* **slurp** *to make noise while eating or drinking*
* **burp** *to pass gas through the mouth*

Comprehension Check

A. Short Answers

Write the answer.

1. Q: How can people make a good impression?
   A: ______________________________

2. Q: What's the seating arrangement like in Asia?
   A: ______________________________

3. Q: What are some things people in parts of Africa avoid when they eat on a carpet?
   A: ______________________________

4. Q: If people in the West stare at you while eating soup, why would they do?
   A: ______________________________

B. Fill in the Blanks

Complete the sentences with the words from the article. Change the form of the words if necessary.

1. It is not polite to ____________ with your mouth open.
2. The seating arrangement is ____________ in some Asian countries.
3. In the West, the seating arrangement often doesn't ____________.
4. In Europe, it is proper to use a new ____________ for each part of the meal.
5. In Japan, it is correct way to eat soup and ramen ____________ loudly.
6. In America, it's not proper to ____________ and chew loudly. It's impolite.
7. When you don't know how to ____________ at the table, you just look to see what other people are doing.

C. True or False

*Check **True** or **False**.*

		True	False
1.	Some manners are followed by people everywhere.	☐	☐
2.	The seating arrangement is pretty simple in Asia.	☐	☐
3.	In the West, the host has to sit at the head of the table.	☐	☐
4.	Start with the tableware farthest from the dish.	☐	☐
5.	Some African people don't worry about whether you can see their feet.	☐	☐
6.	In Japan, you can pick up your bowl off the table.	☐	☐
7.	In China, burping at the table is impolite and rude.	☐	☐
8.	It's important to show respect at the dinner table.	☐	☐

D. Vocabulary Building

Circle the synonym of the word in bold.

1. If someone gives you a present in the West, it is **proper** to open it right away.
   a. fast　　**b.** appropriate
2. In most Asian cultures, you can't eat until the oldest people **lift** their chopsticks.
   a. raise　　**b.** drop
3. Chinese people think it is **rude** to stand your chopsticks up in a bowl of rice.
   a. impolite　　**b.** friendly
4. I am not **sure** what time the meeting starts.
   a. certain　　**b.** wrong

Circle the antonym of the word in bold.

1. It is **polite** to wait until the host says where to sit.
   a. well-behaved　　**b.** cheeky
2. The **noise** outside my window is driving me crazy!
   a. blast　　**b.** silence
3. I didn't sleep well last night. My neighbor was playing music **loudly**.
   a. quietly　　**b.** secretly
4. In Japan, it is **fine** to make slurping sounds when eating ramen.
   a. unacceptable　　**b.** unknown
5. The man was fined $300 for **breaking** a traffic law.
   a. knowing　　**b.** obeying
6. Luckily, the child escaped from the fire with only **minor** injuries.
   a. serious　　**b.** natural

E. Multiple Choice

Circle the answer.

1. How will good manners help you?
   a. People will give you a lot more food.
   b. You'll get a better place to sit at the table.
   c. People will have a good impression on you.
   d. The host will let you sit at the head of the table.

2. Which of the following is true?
   a. Asian people don't care where you sit.
   b. It's fine to lift your bowl in Korea.
   c. Making noise when eating noodles is fine in Japan.
   d. In Europe, eat with the fork closest to the plate first.

3. In Asia, hosts will ...
   a. tell their guests when to eat.
   b. tell their guests where to sit.
   c. sit on a small carpet or a mat.
   d. sit in a seat near the door.

4. What does **those habits** refer to in the fourth paragraph?
   a. slurping soup
   b. eating quietly
   c. burping and chewing loudly
   d. eating on a carpet

Vocabulary Check

A. Word Definitions

Write the words from the article in the appropriate space.

	Word	Definition
1		to bite food several times
2		the way things are organized in a certain order
3		must be obeyed; exact
4		to move something higher
5		to behave in a certain way

B. Meanings in Context

Choose the meaning of the sentence.

1. It's important to **make a good impression** at a job interview.
   a. You need to imitate your interviewer.
   b. You should show people your good points.

2. I'll go to **either** Japan **or** France during the holiday.
   a. I'll go to both Japan and France.
   b. I'll choose one of these two countries.

3. Kim feels uncomfortable when we **stare at** her.
   a. Kim feels strange when we ignore her.
   b. Kim feels strange when we look at her for a long time.

4. **As long as** you practice hard, you will speak French well someday.
   a. If you practice hard, you will speak French well someday.
   b. You don't have to practice hard to speak French well.

C. Words with Different Meanings

Match the word in bold with its definition.

1 It's difficult to book **seats** at that restaurant. ______
The guest was **seated** at the center of the table. ______
Definition: ⓐ *n.* a place to sit ⓑ *v.* to arrange where someone sits

2 There is an important **matter** I need to discuss with you. ______
It doesn't **matter** what your wear. Just wear something comfortable. ______
Definition: ⓐ *v.* to be important ⓑ *n.* a topic

3 I made some **minor** changes to the article. ______
My major is history, and I'm also taking English as my **minor**. ______
Definition: ⓐ *adj.* small and not important ⓑ *n.* the secondary subject someone studies

Reading Strategy

Comparing and Contrasting

TIP

We studied compare and contrast words in Unit 1. Write as many as you can remember in the chart below.

Compare Words	Contrast Words

• Give It a Try •

PART I

Rewrite the sentences with the contrast words given.

1. In Asia, the seating arrangement can be strict. Guests can generally sit where they want in the West. (but)

   ____

   ____

2. In the Middle East, people eat with their hands. Americans use tableware, such as knives, spoons, and forks. (on the other hand)

   ____

   ____

3. In China, people can pick up the bowl and eat rice with chopsticks. Koreans don't lift the bowl and use a spoon to eat rice. (however)

   ____

   ____

PART II

Complete the passage with the words in the box.

just as	like	yet	either

1. ____________ with table manners, drinking customs change from country to country. In South Korea and Japan, never pour your own drink. Russians don't get their own drinks **2.** ____________. They say this is unlucky. If your neighbor empties his or her glass, fill it up for them. In most places, pour drinks using the right hand. Some people say to do this slowly, **3.** ____________ others say it isn't important. When someone of a higher social position gives you a drink, turn away when drinking it. **4.** ____________ in every other part of life, you'll make mistakes. Remember to be polite. Other people will appreciate your effort.

Further Reading

Telling Time Internationally

Track 10

Differences in ideas about time are important when meeting people from different cultures. Words like early and late may mean different things. Some languages may not have words for them at all!

Time Is Money

Americans are probably more concerned with time than any other people. They think wasting time is like wasting money. You should show up at the meeting time and get right down to business.

In Western Europe, time is also important. For business meetings, try to get there about ten minutes early. Arriving about ten minutes late to a friend's home is fine in most countries because it gives your host more time to prepare. However, don't do that in Germany; arriving late is an insult to your host.

Japan is another country that runs "on time." If trains are more than one minute late, they are considered delayed. While the Japanese expect people to be **punctual**, they will not rush through things like meals or meetings.

In South Korea, your social status is important in how punctual you are. If you have a lower status, you must arrive early to wait for the person with a higher status.

Time Is Limitless

India has a slower pace of life and often runs behind schedule because of this. Trains, meetings, and meals can all be late. They have a saying: "Slow is spelled with four letters, so is life. Speed is spelled with five letters, so is death."

South America is similar. People who live there take their time with everything. Showing up an hour late to meet a friend isn't actually late. If you're invited to lunch in Argentina, don't expect a quick meal — they will eat and talk for hours.

People in Africa also have a different view of time. In some parts of East Africa, like Kenya, Swahili speakers tell time by the sunrise and sunset, not by a clock! One hour after sunrise is one in the morning, not 5:00 or 6:00 a.m., so make sure you double-check* when buying a train ticket.

Swahili Time

Swahili time starts at sunrise and finishes at sunset. In the parts of Africa where people speak Swahili, sunrise is usually around 5:00 to 6:00 a.m. Sunset is 7:00 p.m.

Reference:

* **double-check** *to check something again*

Comprehension Check

A. Classification

Write the letter of the country in the blank.

a. USA

b. India

c. Germany

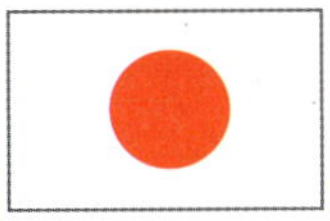
d. Japan

e. Argentina

f. South Korea

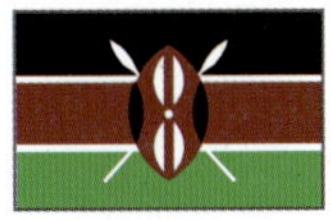
g. Kenya

1. Your host will actually be upset if you arrive late in this European country. ______
2. Trains that arrive more than one minute late are considered delayed. ______
3. You can be less punctual if you have a higher social status. ______
4. Show up for meetings on time and get to work right away. ______
5. Things run slowly in this country. ______
6. If you go to lunch, you won't be able to eat quickly. ______
7. They look at the sky to check the time. ______

B. Fill in the Blanks

Complete the sentences with the words from the article.

1. It is important to aware of differences in ideas about time when we meet people from different ______________.
2. People in America might be more concerned with ______________ than any other people in the world.
3. When you have business meetings in Western Europe, you have to be sure to get there ten minutes ______________.
4. In India, people say ______________ is spelled with five letters, so is death.

C. Multiple Choice

Circle the answer.

1. In the States, people are expected to begin their meeting ...
   - **a.** right away when they meet.
   - **b.** after taking a short break.
   - **c.** whenever they feel like it.
   - **d.** in the afternoon.

2. What is true about people in Western Europe?
   - **a.** They don't like it when you're late for appointments.
   - **b.** They think it's OK to be late to parties.
   - **c.** They will say it's alright to be late for everything.
   - **d.** They don't want you to come early to meetings.

3. What does **punctual** mean in the fourth paragraph?
   - **a.** to be early
   - **b.** to be on time
   - **c.** to be late
   - **d.** to be waiting

4. What is an acceptable time to expect a friend to arrive in South America?
   - **a.** 15 minutes early
   - **b.** on time
   - **c.** a few minutes late
   - **d.** an hour late

UNIT 6 Finding the World's Best with Michelin

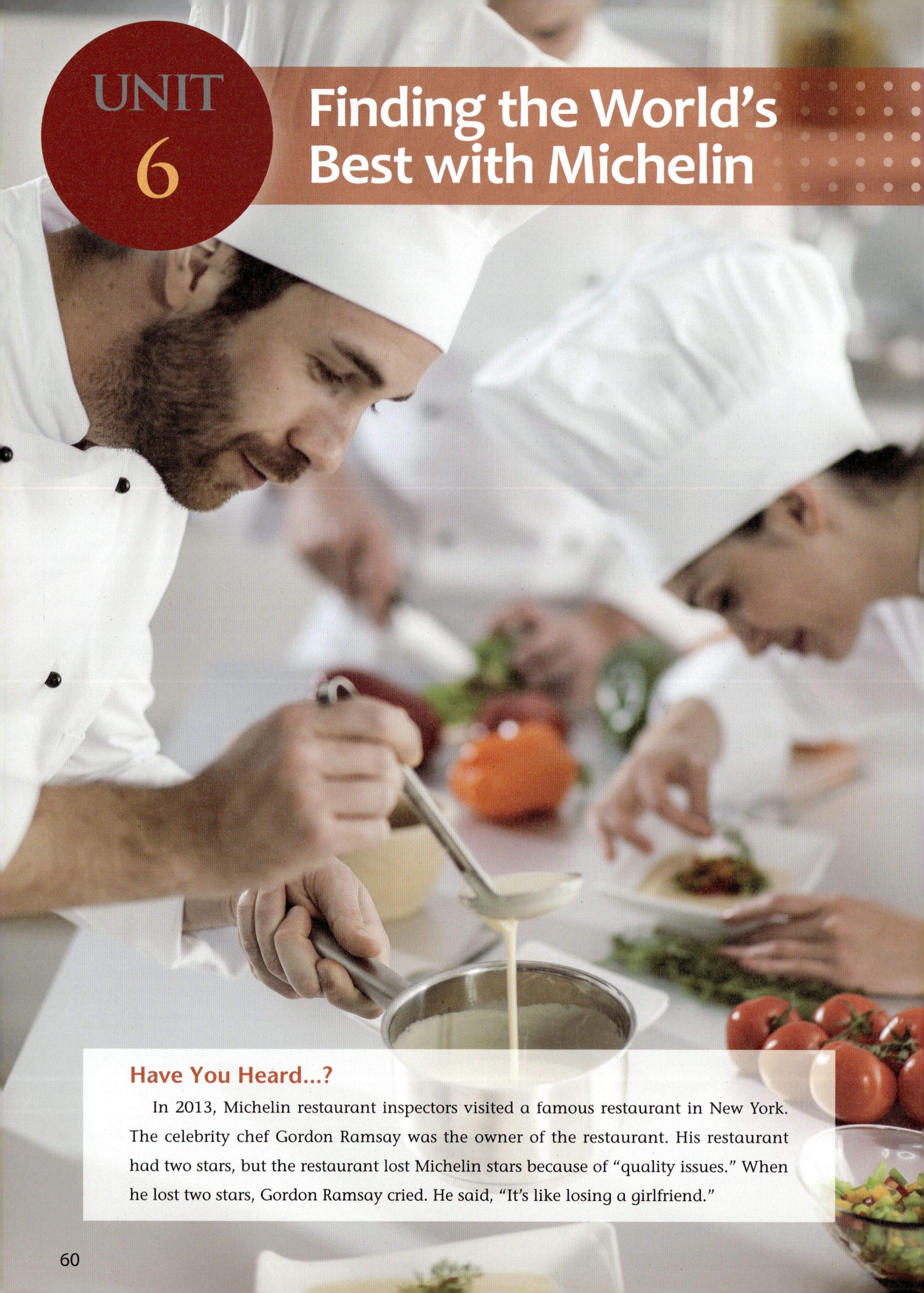

Have You Heard...?

In 2013, Michelin restaurant inspectors visited a famous restaurant in New York. The celebrity chef Gordon Ramsay was the owner of the restaurant. His restaurant had two stars, but the restaurant lost Michelin stars because of "quality issues." When he lost two stars, Gordon Ramsay cried. He said, "It's like losing a girlfriend."

Before We Read

A. Read and Answer

Michelin stars are top **honors** for restaurants. A restaurant can be **rated** between one and three stars. In a Michelin **guidebook**, one star means if the restaurant is on your way, you should stop by. There are 1,900 restaurants in the world that have received one Michelin star. **Worldwide**, 300 restaurants have been given two Michelin stars. These restaurants **deserve** a **detour**. Three-star restaurants are very **rare**. They have **exceptional** food and are worth a special journey.

Write the words in bold above in the appropriate space. Change the form of the words if necessary.

	Word	Definition		Word	Definition
1		should get	2		a book of information
3		not common	4		everywhere in the world
5		a longer route	6		to grade something
7		very good	8		great esteem

B. Make Predictions

Read the first sentence of each paragraph on pages 62 and 63. Answer the questions.

1. What do you think the reading is about?
   - ☐ the story of a tire company
   - ☐ the history of the *Michelin Guide*
   - ☐ how to make your restaurant better
   - ☐ the most popular restaurant in the world

2. Which of the following won't be included in the article?
   - ☐ the restaurants Michelin does not like at all
   - ☐ why Michelin reviews have become famous
   - ☐ what makes the *Michelin Guide* seem special
   - ☐ Michelin's special way of rating restaurants

TIP
The first sentence of a paragraph *explains the main idea to follow. It normally focuses on places, time, comparing or contrasting, listing, and general details.*

C. Scan

Read the article again. What do the following numbers refer to?

a. the amount of restaurants with the highest rating
b. when Michelin started giving information on restaurants
c. the number of countries with *Michelin Guidebooks*

1. 1900 _____ **2.** 71 _____ **3.** 20 _____

Michelin: Your Guide to Fine Dining

Track 11

Michelin has been in business for more than a century. The company sells tires, but in 1900, it began publishing guidebooks with information for drivers, such as where to stay, where to eat, and where to get gas.

Over the years, Michelin has become famous for its restaurant reviews. People worldwide believe that Michelin reviews are the best in the world. After all, their guidebooks are published in over 20 countries.

So, how is the Michelin Guide different from other restaurant and hotel guidebooks? For one thing, no one is supposed to know who works for Michelin. For another, no one knows when a Michelin employee will stop by. This is because Michelin believes that sending a secret inspector to a restaurant is the only way to get an honest review. If the inspector likes the restaurant, he or she will rate it with one to three stars and it is included in the guidebook. The more stars a restaurant earns, the better it is. Michelin doesn't hand out stars easily though. There are only 71 restaurants in the world that have three stars.

A rating from Michelin might make a restaurant really popular, but sometimes it can mean trouble for restaurant owners. One famous French chef,* for example, loved his Michelin stars so much that he killed himself when he learned his restaurant had lost a star.

In addition, people who use Michelin guidebooks go a little crazy. Some of them spend all their money going to Michelin restaurants because they believe they are going to the best of the best. To them, a visit to a restaurant with Michelin stars is guaranteed to be a delicious adventure.

Reference:
* **chef** *the main cook at a restaurant or hotel*

Comprehension Check

A. True or False

*Check **True** or **False**.*

	True	False
1. Michelin is over 100 years old.	☐	☐
2. People in lots of countries read Michelin's reviews.	☐	☐
3. Michelin inspectors openly visit different restaurants.	☐	☐
4. Michelin inspectors give stars easily.	☐	☐
5. A cook in France killed himself after receiving a rating he didn't like.	☐	☐

B. Reference Word

Choose what the word in bold refers to.

1. ... **it** began publishing guidebooks with information ... where to get gas. (Paragraph 1)
   a. a gas company　　**b.** a tire company
   c. a restaurant　　**d.** a guide

2. After all, **their** guidebooks are published in over 20 countries. (Paragraph 2)
   a. Michelin　　**b.** drivers
   c. Hong Kong　　**d.** French restaurants

3. If the inspector ... **it** is included in the guidebook. (Paragraph 3)
   a. one star to three stars　　**b.** the inspector
   c. the place the inspector visits　　**d.** a Michelin employee

4. ... but sometimes **it** can mean trouble for restaurant owners. (Paragraph 4)
   a. a Michelin review　　**b.** a guidebook
   c. a famous French chef　　**d.** an employee

5. Some of **them** spend all their ... best of the best. (Paragraph 5)
   a. drivers　　**b.** Michelin guidebook followers
   c. delicious meals　　**d.** the best restaurants

C. Make Inferences

Match the sentence with its inference.

> **a.** Michelin is a successful company.
> **b.** Getting a star is important to some restaurant owners.
> **c.** Restaurant owners can't pay for good ratings.

1. Michelin has been in business for more than a century. _____
2. No one knows when a Michelin employee will stop by. _____
3. One famous chef killed himself when he learned his restaurant had lost a star. _____

D. Vocabulary Building

Circle the synonym of the word in bold.

1. The **company** I work at has been publishing books for a long time.
   a. firm b. station
2. Kerry isn't going to buy a car that runs on **gas**. She'll get an electric-powered one this time.
   a. fuel b. batteries
3. Everyone comes to this restaurant. It's **famous**.
   a. well-known b. unknown
4. We have over 200 **employees** working in our factory.
   a. bosses b. workers

Circle the antonym of the word in bold.

1. Although Jack and Ray are twins, their personalities are **different**.
   a. similar b. contrasting
2. Andy **earned** a lot of money investing in the stock market.
   a. gathered b. lost
3. This soup is **delicious**. You'll love it.
   a. fabulous b. tasteless
4. Angela is recognized as the **best** in her field.
   a. terrible b. top

E. Multiple Choice

Circle the answer.

1. When did Michelin start publishing guidebooks?
   a. since 20th century
   b. just recently
   c. 71 years ago
   d. It doesn't say.

2. What in NOT included in Michelin guide when it was first published?
   a. where to stay
   b. where to get gas
   c. where to buy souvenirs
   d. where to eat

3. Restaurants with more stars have ...
   a. better reputations.
   b. higher prices.
   c. more employees.
   d. more locations.

4. Sometimes a rating from Michelin is highly influential for ...
   a. inspectors.
   b. drivers.
   c. restaurant owners.
   d. hotel employees.

5. Which of the following is NOT true?
   a. People could get Michelin reviews everywhere.
   b. Michelin is only famous for its hotel reviews.
   c. Almost nobody knows when an inspector is coming.
   d. Some people really care about getting a Michelin star.

Vocabulary Check

A. Fill in the Missing Letters

Complete the sentences with the words from the article.

1. The airplane was invented at the beginning of the last **c**__________. (paragraph 1)
2. The **g**__________ says this is the best restaurant in the city. (paragraph 1)
3. His latest novel received mostly rave **r**__________. (paragraph 2)
4. The first Harry Potter book was **p**__________ in 1997. (paragraph 2)
5. Pamela is a reliable **e**__________. She never misses work. (paragraph 3)
6. We did a good job building this tower. The **i**__________ will like it. (paragraph 3)
7. The cost of the food is **i**__________ in the price. (paragraph 3)
8. My grandfather used to tell us about his **a**__________ as a sailor. (paragraph 5)

B. Words with Different Meanings

Match the word in bold with its definition.

1
Details of how to use the machine are in the user's **guide**. ______
The man **guided** us through the narrow streets to the hotel. ______
Definition: ⓐ *n.* instructions ⓑ *v.* to lead

2
The restaurant has had good **reviews**. ______
Heather's job is to **review** books for the local newspaper. ______
Definition: ⓐ *v.* to give an opinion about something ⓑ *n.* an opinion about something

3
The salesman **guaranteed** my mother that she was buying a first-rate car. ______
This camera comes with a one-month **guarantee**. ______
Definition: ⓐ *v.* to promise something ⓑ *n.* a promise of something

C. Meanings in Context

Choose the meaning of the phrase in bold.

1. The company has been **in business** for over 20 years.
   - **a.** operating a company
   - **b.** following business news

2. We **are supposed to** arrive at the airport by 11 o'clock.
   - **a.** could
   - **b.** should

3. Prizes are **handed out** every year to the two students with the highest grades.
   - **a.** given
   - **b.** taken from

4. Every time I go to the mall, I **go** a little **crazy** and buy too much stuff.
   - **a.** become depressed
   - **b.** become excited

Reading Strategy

Separating Facts from Opinions

TIP

A fact is something that can be proven, while an opinion is someone's ideas or beliefs about something. If the writer says something general, such as Everyone knows..., he or she is probably giving an opinion. Here are some common phrases for expressing opinions.

I believe / feel / think ...	... is better than ...	... is the best ...
In my opinion	In my point of view	

- **Fact:** The wall was painted last summer, on August 1st.
- **Opinion:** That is the best painting job ever.

• Give It a Try •

PART I

*Check **Fact** or **Opinion**.*

	Fact	Opinion
1. Michelin has been in business for more than a century.	☐	☐
2. Some people believe that Michelin reviews are the best in the world.	☐	☐
3. Michelin guidebooks are published in over 20 countries.	☐	☐
4. There are 71 restaurants in the world that have three Michelin stars.	☐	☐
5. One famous French chef killed himself when he lost a Michelin star.	☐	☐
6. Restaurants with Michelin stars are the best of the best.	☐	☐
7. Some people think that Michelin reviews are reliable.	☐	☐

PART II

Underline the words in the sentences that make them opinions. Give your reasons.

1. The whole world cares about the upcoming Olympics.
2. Nobody is ever going to read this book. It's terrible.
3. Whenever people travel, they feel excited.
4. I think Jenny's new coat looks great on her.
5. She always says Michael Jackson was the best musician.
6. In my opinion, you'd better leave now.
7. Jason looks much better than his picture.

Further Reading

The Men and Women Behind the Michelin Guide

Track 12

Do you think you have what it takes to be a Michelin inspector? Michelin inspectors are masters in disguise, and they work hard to keep their identity a secret. A Michelin inspector could be anyone. They act like regular customers while doing their jobs. They aren't allowed to tell anyone about their work, including their family. Even some of Michelin's top employees have never met an inspector!

Besides keeping secrets, Michelin inspectors need to enjoy traveling. You'll have to be prepared to travel at least 25,000 miles and visit around 1,000 restaurants each year. Most importantly, you must understand food. Inspectors normally have ten or more years of experience in the hotel and restaurant industry. Instead of simple dishes like soups and salads, they usually order meals that are difficult to cook and include a number of ingredients. Then, they write about every detail, such as the method of cooking, taste, wine, and even the way the table is set and served.

Inspectors rate their favorite restaurants in two ways. Each restaurant is rated on its level of comfort. A score of five is high, while a score of one is low. If an inspector really likes a restaurant, he or she can give it a special award called the Bib Gourmand.* These awards are given out to restaurants that offer excellent food and service for a great price.

Michelin inspectors understand food and the restaurant business. They enjoy traveling all over the country and eating out regularly. Most importantly, they are good at keeping secrets. If you have these qualities, you can become a Michelin inspector, too.

Reference:

* **gourmand** *someone who's interested in good food and drink*

Comprehension Check

A. Details

Check the answers.

What does it take to become a Michelin inspector?

- ☐ Besides your family, you won't tell anyone about your job.
- ☐ Sometimes, you'll need to pretend to be someone you're not.
- ☐ You will have to have lots of patience when it comes to traveling.
- ☐ You need to work in a restaurant and hotel first before taking this job.
- ☐ Inspectors need to know people who work at expensive restaurants.

B. Summary

Choose the answer.

Becoming a Michelin **1.** ____________ isn't as easy as it looks. First of all, you have to be a master in disguise. People shouldn't be able to find out your **2.** ____________; nobody should know your job, not even your family. Inspectors usually need at least ten years of experience in the food industry. They must write about every **3.** ____________ while checking out a restaurant, including the cooking, taste, wine, and service. The level of **4.** ____________ a restaurant offers is important too. Finally, inspectors need to be fair. They should try to understand the different kinds of food people like in the countries they **5.** ____________. This is also part of the job.

1.	**a.** editor	**b.** checker	**c.** inspector	**d.** reader
2.	**a.** age	**b.** hometown	**c.** identity	**d.** source
3.	**a.** recipe	**b.** detail	**c.** basic	**d.** idea
4.	**a.** comfort	**b.** comfortable	**c.** comfortless	**d.** comforting
5.	**a.** alive	**b.** depart	**c.** live	**d.** visit

C. Multiple Choice

Circle the answer.

1. Michelin inspectors do all of the following BUT ...
   a. write about the details of a restaurant.
   b. act just like any other normal customer.
   c. introduce themselves to Michelin workers.
   d. give great restaurants a rating using stars.

2. How many restaurants do Michelin inspectors review yearly?
   a. 25,000
   b. 1,000
   c. less than 100
   d. a couple of restaurants

3. Why do Michelin inspectors NOT order soups or salads?
   a. They are expensive.
   b. They are easy to make.
   c. They don't taste good.
   d. They have too many ingredients.

4. What is the reading mainly about?
   a. restaurants in Asia receiving Michelin stars
   b. what Michelin inspectors usually eat
   c. how to keep a secret for a long time
   d. the life and job of a Michelin inspector

UNIT 7

Music Is in Our Soul

Have You Heard...?

- Stress is reduced by 41 percent when people listen to fast music.
- Slow music increases drink sales by 40 percent and influences customers to stay 24 percent longer.
- Supermarkets earn 38 percent more money when they play easy-listening music.
- Sales increase 11.6 percent when fast music is played during lunch hour; sales go up 15.7 percent when slower music is played at dinnertime.
- Workers improve output by ten percent when they listen to music.

Before We Read

A. Read and Answer

In addition to helping us to relax and providing **enjoyment**, music has a lot of other amazing **effects**. For example, Thomas Jefferson used music as a tool while writing America's Declaration of Independence. When he **ran out of** ideas, he would play his violin to help him find the right words. Albert Einstein **appeared** to know the **benefits** of music too. When he was young, he didn't do well at school. In fact, his teacher said he was "too stupid to learn." However, Mozart and Bach's **classical** music helped Einstein become one of the smartest men in history.

Write the words/phrases in bold above in the appropriate space. Change the form of the words if necessary.

	Word/Phrase	Definition
1		to have nothing left
2		an advantage
3		relating to music from the past
4		to seem
5		a result
6		the feeling of happiness

B. Make Predictions

Read the first and the last paragraphs on pages 72 and 73. What does the title probably mean?

- ☐ the earliest pieces of music known to us
- ☐ finding a good tool by listening to music
- ☐ the power of music to influence us
- ☐ a way to play the best music

TIP
__The first paragraph__ of an article introduces the overall idea. __The final paragraph__ emphasizes this point. If you have trouble understanding the first paragraph, try reading the last one.

C. Scan

Read the article again. Music has all of the following effects BUT ...

- ☐ to make people feel relaxed.
- ☐ to make people want to become dentists.
- ☐ to make chickens lay bigger eggs.
- ☐ to increase some animals' output.
- ☐ to help people pay attention.
- ☐ to increase a person's appetite.
- ☐ to ease patients when they are uncomfortable.
- ☐ to help plants grow in certain ways.

Powerful Beats

Track 13

Music has been important to humans for as long as we can remember. The earliest known music was written on a tablet 15,000 years ago. Researchers have even found flutes that are 50,000 years old. Besides being for enjoyment, music is used as a tool.

Psychologists write about the benefits of music. For example, it helps people relax. Research shows that stress can be reduced by over 40 percent. Music also helps us concentrate. Studies find that workers do ten percent more work when they are listening to music. Not surprisingly, only specific kinds of music have this effect. Music that has a tempo* of 60 beats per minute, like classical Baroque music, is best.

Music also makes us eat and drink more. Scientists now know that fast music makes us eat faster, and slow music makes us eat longer. If you eat fast, your body doesn't have time to tell you it's full and you often eat too much. If you eat for a long time, you're likely to order extra desserts or drinks. For this reason, many restaurants will play classical music in the background. It has helped to increase drink sales by 40 percent and gotten customers to stay 24 percent longer than they usually would.

Most people admit to being nervous going into the dentist's office. No one likes the sounds of a drill working on their teeth. A dentist and psychologist worked together to see if playing classical music would comfort patients. Patients who listened to classical music in headphones had a more relaxing experience than those who did not.

Humans aren't the only ones affected by music. Classical music makes chickens lay more eggs and cows produce more milk. Even plants appear to respond to music: plants in a room with classical music blossom and grow toward the music; plants in a room with rock music dry up and die.

Music is great as both a source of entertainment and a tool. Classical music has the power to improve not only your grades, but also your chickens' output. That sounds like good news!

Reference:

* **tempo** *the speed at which music is played*

Comprehension Check

A. Fill in the Missing Letters

Complete the sentences with the words from the article. Change the form of the words if necessary.

1. Music can be for more than just enjoyment. It can be used as a **t**____________.
2. Research indicates that music helps people relax and **c**____________ better.
3. Music with a tempo of 60 **b**____________ per minute, like classical Baroque music, is the most helpful for workers.
4. A lot of restaurants play classical music in the **b**____________ as this might lead customers to order more drinks.
5. It seems that humans are not the only ones **a**____________ by music.
6. Plants near classical music **b**____________ and even grow in the direction of the music.

B. True or False

*Check **True** or **False**.*

		True	False
1.	Music has been important to people for many years.	☐	☐
2.	Research hasn't shown that music helps people reduce their stress.	☐	☐
3.	Scientists believe that workers work harder when they listen to music.	☐	☐
4.	Slow music makes people eat faster.	☐	☐
5.	Slow music makes customers stay longer in a restaurant.	☐	☐
6.	Patients listening to classical music feel more comfortable.	☐	☐
7.	Classical music helps chickens to produce more eggs.	☐	☐
8.	Plants aren't influenced by music.	☐	☐

C. Make Inferences

Match the sentence with its inference.

- **a.** Research shows us how music helps us do better in school.
- **b.** Music that has a faster beat will often make us do things more quickly.
- **c.** The dentist's drill sounds terrible.
- **d.** Some farmers play classical music near their chickens.
- **e.** Our love of music comes to us naturally.

1. Music has been important to humans for as long as we can remember. _____
2. Psychologists write about the benefits of music. _____
3. Scientists now know that fast music makes us eat faster, and slow music makes us eat longer. _____
4. No one likes the sounds of a drill working on their teeth. _____
5. Classical music makes chickens lay more eggs. _____

D. Vocabulary Building

Circle the synonym of the word/phrase in bold.

1. Calcium is **important** for the development of teeth and bones.
   a. harmful　　b. essential
2. Lily gets a lot of **enjoyment** out of teaching young children.
   a. pleasure　　b. tears
3. I'm looking for a **specific** type of drink. It's cherry flavored.
   a. particular　　b. normal
4. You look a little **nervous**. Why don't you take a deep breath and try to calm down?
   a. relaxed　　b. tense
5. Lucy sang a song to **comfort** the crying baby.
   a. soothe　　b. amuse
6. Advertisements **affect** our shopping behavior and habits.
   a. influence　　b. remove
7. The actors in the 3D movie **appeared to** be real.
   a. tried to　　b. seemed to
8. Evelyn **responded** angrily to Nick's suggestion.
   a. behaved　　b. reacted

E. Multiple Choice

Circle the answer.

1. How long have we been listening to music?
   a. just a few centuries ago
   b. for only 15,000 years
   c. for a very short time
   d. as long as we can remember

2. Why is listening to music good for people under pressure?
   a. Music helps them release their stress.
   b. They can learn something new.
   c. Music is very emotional.
   d. The tempo of music is quite fast.

3. How does slow music help restaurant owners?
   a. Their customers leave sooner.
   b. Their customers eat more quietly.
   c. Their customers order more drinks.
   d. Their customers feel less stress.

4. Classical music makes people in a dental clinic ...
   a. use the drill.
   b. take it easy.
   c. get excited.
   d. understand the dentists more.

5. What is the reading mainly about?
   a. all of the great research scientists are doing
   b. the sound of classical music in the future
   c. what music is doing to our society now
   d. how we are influenced by music

Vocabulary Check

A. Complete the Sentences

Fill in the blanks with the words in the box. Change the form of the words if necessary.

tablet	background	nervous	blossom	source

1. Cindy is ______________ about her interview next week. She hasn't slept well for days.
2. Before paper was invented, people wrote on stone or clay ______________.
3. The Internet is a useful ______________ of information.
4. In southern Japan, cherry trees start to ______________ as early as January.
5. The ______________ sound was so loud that I couldn't hear you at all.

B. Words in Context

Choose the answer.

1. I can never **concentrate**. I just can't think carefully / lazily about problems.
2. The courses are not designed for **specific** age groups. They're suitable for everyone / a certain group.
3. The man finally **admitted to** murdering his neighbor. He refused / told the police everything about the crime.
4. As sunlight increases **output**, chickens produce a larger amount / size of eggs in summer.

C. Words with Different Meanings

Match the word in bold with its definition.

1. Jessica danced to the **beat** of the music. ______
   I always **beat** my brother at chess. ______
   Definition: ⓐ *n.* rhythm ⓑ *v.* to defeat

2. You're going to need a **drill** to make a hole in the wall. ______
   You need a license to **drill** for oil in the area. ______
   Definition: ⓐ *v.* to make a hole ⓑ *n.* a tool or machine used for making holes

3. There is a lot of research being done on the care for cancer **patients**. ______
   You'll just have to be **patient** and wait for Matt to finish his explanation. ______
   Definition: ⓐ *n.* a sick person ⓑ *adj.* calmly waiting for a long time

D. Word Formation

*Fill in the blanks to make words using the suffixes **–ist** and **–ment**.*

–ist	• ______________ist (a person who studies the human mind) • ______________ist (a person who works in science) • ______________ist (a person who treats people's teeth)
–ment	• enjoy (verb) → ______________ (noun) • entertain (verb) → ______________ (noun) • improve (verb) → ______________ (noun)

Reading Strategy

Identifying Supporting Details

TIP

Paragraphs begin with a topic sentence to explain the most important point. The topic sentence is supported by facts and statistics. Statistics are helpful in getting the reader to understand the main idea. Many readers think statistics are true — that they are not the writer's opinions.

• Give It a Try •

PART I

*Check **Fact, Statistic,** or **Opinion.***

	Fact	Statistic	Opinion
1. The earliest known music was written on a tablet 15,000 years ago.	☐	☐	☐
2. Researchers have found flutes that are 50,000 years old.	☐	☐	☐
3. It is possible to use music as a tool in your life.	☐	☐	☐
4. Psychologists write about the benefits of music.	☐	☐	☐
5. Researches show that stress can be reduced by over 40 percent.	☐	☐	☐
6. Studies find that workers do ten percent more work when they are listening to music.	☐	☐	☐
7. Scientists now know that fast music makes us eat faster, and slow music makes us eat longer.	☐	☐	☐
8. Most people admit to being nervous going into the dentist's office.	☐	☐	☐

PART II

Write S if the sentence supports the main idea or NS if it doesn't.

San Francisco is a great city to visit.

_____ It's always sunny there, but not too hot.
_____ The baseball team is terrible. They never win.
_____ The city has many great places to spend the afternoon, like Chinatown, Fisherman's Wharf, or the San Francisco Zoo.
_____ The famous prison, called Alcatraz, closed down in the early 1960s.
_____ There are lots of great international restaurants.

***Casablanca* is one of the greatest films ever made.**

_____ The actors and actresses are wonderful.
_____ The stars of *Casablanca* were paid a lot of money.
_____ *Casablanca*'s music is beautiful. The song *As Time Goes By* is great.
_____ *Casablanca* was filmed in Hollywood, not Africa.
_____ The story is both romantic and meaningful.

Further Reading

The Power of Music

Track 14

People are sitting in front of the TV and a commercial comes on. There are children with sad faces. There are images of destroyed lands. The words appear: You can help. People, however, aren't interested in the commercial, and the commercial doesn't raise much money. The screen goes black and the same commercial comes on again. This time it comes with hopeful music. People become interested in the ad. They see images of volunteers helping smiling children. The same words appear: You can help. People stare at the screen for a while and reach for their credit card. According to researchers, the images alone would not have produced the same response in people. When there are images without music, the ad doesn't make sense. Then people don't donate. However, when there is hopeful music with the words, there is an increase in the amount of money raised.

Studies have shown that music influences people's feelings. Big companies and small charities use this information to design their commercials. In the past, commercials mainly used words and images, but these days advertisers pay attention to music much more. Music affects how people think about a brand, so companies use music in commercials to deliver their message more effectively. Viewers receive the message more positively when there is music. Different music is used to appeal to different target groups as well. Classical music might appeal to an older audience, while pop songs could reach a younger crowd.

Music also affects memory. Many adults say that they remember commercials from their childhood. Years after they first watched, the songs from commercials stick with them. They remember the commercials because the music in the commercial triggered the memory. Researchers found that it is easier to remember information when it appears with music than without music. For example, imagine you see an ad for ice cream that includes music. Then when you go shopping, you hear the music in the store. The music triggers your memory and makes you automatically conjure up the image of ice cream. Finally, you reach for the ice cream.

Next time you watch an advertisement, pay attention to the music. Is it fast or slow? How does it make you feel? When music makes the ad memorable, you are more likely to buy the product.

Comprehension Check

A. Fill in the Missing Letters

Complete the sentences with the words from the article. Change the form of the words if necessary.

1. In the past, commercials **m**__________ used words and images only.
2. The city and surrounding lands are **d**__________ by the war.
3. Music is used by advertisers from big **c**__________.
4. Viewers receive the **m**__________ that music delivers in commercials.
5. People can remember commercials from their childhood because the music in commercials brings back their **m**__________.
6. Music makes advertisements **m**__________.

B. True or False

*Check **True** or **False**.*

	True	False
1. Charities never use music in their commercials.	☐	☐
2. Music influences the way people feel.	☐	☐
3. Music helps people remember a product.	☐	☐
4. The images without music have more influence than with music.	☐	☐
5. Advertisers paid attention to music much more in the past.	☐	☐
6. People's memories are affected by music.	☐	☐
7. Some people remember music from ads for many years.	☐	☐
8. Music delivers a message to viewers.	☐	☐

C. Multiple Choice

Circle the answer.

1. Which of the following is NOT influenced by music?
   - a. memory
   - b. feelings
   - c. attitude to a brand
   - d. information about products

2. In commercials, viewers receive a message __________ when there is music.
   - a. hopefully
   - b. hardly
   - c. positively
   - d. slowly

3. People are more likely to remember advertisements with music because ...
   - a. music makes them sad.
   - b. there is no music.
   - c. music triggered the memory.
   - d. they are full of information.

4. Which conclusion can we make after reading the article?
   - a. Music makes children sad.
   - b. Music used in advertising can affect sales.
   - c. Music in advertisements is easy to forget.
   - d. Music affects everyone in the same way.

UNIT 8 Work Not as You Know It

Have You Heard...?

In 1965, ama divers earned $85,000,000. The average age for an ama diver was 67. Amas were also heroes of pop culture. Their faces were on stamps and posters. In the James Bond movie *You Only Live Twice*, 007 was attracted to a beautiful ama diver. With global warming, ama diving is becoming less common. This is sad news for Japan. The custom has been an important part of Japanese society for 1,500 years.

Before We Read

A. Make Predictions

Read the title and the subtitles on pages 82 and 83. What do you think the reading is about?

- ☐ attacks by hackers
- ☐ learning to cook
- ☐ job application
- ☐ unusual jobs
- ☐ people using SNS
- ☐ career advice

B. Read and Answer

Read the article on pages 82 and 83. Write the job title in the blank to match each ad.

1. ______________

Looking for an experienced **social media** user familiar with a variety of platforms such as Facebook, Twitter, Instagram, and blogs. Job includes following social media mentions of our company and providing **feedback**. Marketing experience is a plus.

2. ______________

It's more than food. It's art! Seeking an experienced cook who understands the value of well-presented food. Must be able to select, purchase, cook and arrange food for photo shoots. **Creativity** is required.

3. ______________

Are you interested in computers? Have you studied computer science? Our company is looking for **security** experts to join the team of the best hackers in the world. Training is provided.

Use the words in bold above to complete the sentences.

1. I use ______________ a lot - Facebook, Twitter, Pinterest, and WhatsApp.
2. Alica is an artist. I am impressed by her ______________.
3. Do you think this is good or bad? I need your ______________.
4. Our home ______________ system includes CCTV.

Cool Careers

Track 15

Professional Hacker

Jeremiah Grossman is a professional hacker. When he was 18 years old, he enjoyed breaking computer software for fun. The CEOs of Yahoo! discovered him when he anonymously sent them an email explaining vulnerabilities in their system. They offered him a job hacking all their software to discover the problems. With his help, they became less vulnerable. Later, Grossman went into business for himself, WhiteHat Security. His company is an army of hackers who work as consultants to large companies to discover problems in their security systems. He trains computer science majors to become hackers for his company. His workers become some of the best hackers protecting the world from Black Hats — the bad hackers. Professional hackers have a fast-paced, exciting job.

Food Stylist

Annie Hudson is a food stylist. Food stylists work with art directors and photographers in a commercial food studio to shoot food photographs. They create real food for anything from cookbooks to TV commercials. A food stylist first has to be a good cook. They cook all their food at the studio, so it is fresh. However, looks are more important than taste in a food shoot, so the stylist uses some tricks to make the food look camera perfect. Using cream instead of milk makes cereal look more appetizing. Blowing hot air through a straw melts ice cream just right. Lipstick makes strawberries red! A food stylist buys the ingredients, makes the food, and perfectly arranges it for its big moment. It is a job that combines cooking skills and creativity.

Chief Listening Officer

Beth LaPierre is Kodak's Chief Listening Officer (CLO). What is a CLO? It is a person whose job is to be online all day, looking out for mentions of their company's products on social media like blogs, Facebook, Twitter, Instagram and other programs. As people use social media more and more to complain about companies or brag about good deals, it is becoming more and more important for companies to have someone who listens for that valuable feedback. A CLO has three important tasks. They listen to the customers and understand what they are saying. Then they give the important information to the right people inside the company. Finally, they let the customers know that they are listening. CLOs love the internet and interacting with people online.

How about you? Whether you love to use the computer, love to cook, or something else, the important thing is to find a job that matches your interests.

Comprehension Check

A. Fill in the Missing Letters

Complete the sentences with the words from the article. Change the form of the words if necessary.

1. Hackers discover problems in **s**____________ systems of large companies.
2. Hackers can find problems in software and then make it less **v**____________.
3. Food stylists can **c**____________ beautiful arrangements of food from cookbooks.
4. A food stylist purchases the **i**____________, makes the food, and arranges it for a photo shoot.
5. Using cream instead of milk makes cereal appear more **a**____________ in a photo.
6. CLOs enjoy **i**____________ with people online.
7. Listening, giving feedback, and interacting are three important **t**____________ of a CLO.
8. People would like to use Facebook to **b**____________ about good deals.

B. Classification

Match the sentence with its type of job.

a. professional hacker	**b.** food stylist	**c.** chief listening officer

1. They are good cooks. ______
2. They find the weaknesses in computer software of big firms. ______
3. They use tricks to make the food beautiful. ______
4. This job is good for someone who spends a lot of time online. ______
5. This job is not good for someone who doesn't understand computers. ______
6. Computer science majors are better at this job. ______
7. People with good communication skills are good at this job. ______

C. Reference Word

Choose what the word in bold refers to.

1. His company is an army of hackers who work as consultants to large companies to discover problems in **their** security systems. (paragraph 1)
   a. computer scientists **b.** companies
   c. Jeremiah Grossman **d.** consultants
2. With his help, **they** became less vulnerable. (paragraph 1)
   a. consultants **b.** security systems
   c. computer science majors **d.** hackers
3. **They** create real food for anything from cookbooks to TV commercials. (paragraph 2)
   a. photographers **b.** art directors
   c. food stylists **d.** studios
4. They listen to the customers and understand what **they** are saying. (paragraph 3)
   a. chief listening officers **b.** customers
   c. companies **d.** social media

D. Vocabulary Building

Circle the synonym of the word in bold.

1. John didn't want to use his name, so he left the letter **anonymous**.
   a. signed　　b. unsigned
2. Sara has a **fast-paced** lifestyle. She is always so busy.
   a. slow　　b. quickly changing
3. The strawberries are so red. They look really **appetizing**.
   a. delicious　　b. awful
4. Alica's artwork is special. She has so much **creativity**.
   a. boredom　　b. imagination
5. Tom's sister **bragged** about her expensive new computer.
   a. hid　　b. talked
6. My brother is very shy. He doesn't like to **interact** with strangers.
   a. separate　　b. communicate

E. Multiple Choice

Circle the answer.

1. What is NOT true about Jeremian Grossman?
   a. He enjoyed hacking software when he was a teenager.
   b. He was offered a job from Yahoo!
   c. He made problems in security systems of big companies.
   d. He found a company which is an army of good hackers.

2. What is true about hackers?
   a. They have a boring job.
   b. They are not very good at computers.
   c. They don't help companies with security.
   d. They sometimes work as consultants to large companies.

3. Why do food stylists have to be good cooks?
   a. They work with art directors and photographers.
   b. They have to eat the food they create.
   c. They cook all their food at the studio before shoot.
   d. Taste is more important than looks.

4. What kind of people should become chief listening officers?
   a. People who don't like spending time on the computer.
   b. People who like interacting with others online.
   c. People who are not good listeners.
   d. People who want a fast-paced lifestyle.

5. What can we infer from the last paragraph?
   a. Everyone should work just for the money.
   b. It is more important to find a job that you like to do.
   c. Using the computer is interesting to everyone.
   d. Your interests are not very important when you are looking for a job.

Vocabulary Check

A. Word Definitions

Write the words from the article in the appropriate space. Change the form of the words if necessary.

	Word	Career	Definition
1		food stylist	appealing, makes you want to eat it
2		CLO	reference to something or someone
3		Professional Hacker	a person who provides expert advice
4		CLO	information about reaction to something
5		food stylist	a person who arranges things in a beautiful way
6		Professional Hacker	happening quickly
7		food stylist	to take photographs using a camera
8		Professional Hacker	easy to hurt

B. Words in Context

Choose the answer.

1. He sent the email **anonymously**.
   → He sent the email with his name / without his name.
2. The company uses **commercials** to advertise their products.
   → The company advertises their products on TV / in the pool.
3. Sandra **bragged** about the high score she got on her exam.
   → Sandra told people / didn't tell anyone about her score.
4. Mark's boss gave him a **task** to do before he went home.
   → Mark's boss gave him work / summer vacation before he went home.
5. People who spend a lot of time on social media enjoy **interacting** with others.
   → People who spend a lot of time on social media enjoy talking to / ignoring other people.

TIP
*We often add –**ing** or –**ed** to verbs to make adjectives.*

C. Fill in the Blanks

Use the words in bold to complete the sentences.

1. All of these activities **bore** me. My friends find them ______________ too.
2. Public speaking **frightens** many people. They are too ______________ to speak in front of people in public.
3. Grammar rules **confuse** me. Verbs and adjectives are so ______________.
4. The news **surprised** him. He told it to his family. They thought it was quite ______________ as well.

Reading Strategy

Understanding Cause and Effect

TIP

We introduced cause and effect words in Unit 2. List the words you can remember and put them in the appropriate box.

Followed by CAUSE	Followed by EFFECT

• Give It a Try •

PART I

Match the cause and effect.

Effect

a. Companies hire CLO to find out what the public is saying about them.
b. CLOs give important information to the company.
c. Yahoo! became less vulnerable.
d. It is very fresh.
e. They offered him a job.

Cause

1. Jeremiah Grossman sent Yahoo! an anonymous email. ______
2. People use social media to complain about products. ______
3. Food stylists cook all their food at the studio. ______
4. Grossman agreed to work for Yahoo! ______
5. Companies want to listen what the public is saying about them. ______

PART II

Choose the answer.

The ocean's coral reefs are being affected in many ways. We know that some of the damage is a **1.** ______________ of human activity. Throwing garbage and other waste products into the water **2.** ______________ changes to the environment. **3.** ______________ these changes, the ocean has become polluted. **4.** ______________, coral reefs are being destroyed. Coral reefs are being damaged faster than ever before. **5.** ______________ we need to be more serious about this problem.

1.	**a.** led	**b.** rise	**c.** result	**d.** due
2.	**a.** occurs	**b.** leaves	**c.** causes	**d.** leads
3.	**a.** Because	**b.** Because of	**c.** Since	**d.** As
4.	**a.** As a result	**b.** Since	**c.** When	**d.** In view of
5.	**a.** However	**b.** Therefore	**c.** Furthermore	**d.** Because

Further Reading

Internships on a Farm

Track 16

Many young people are choosing to try living and working on farms for a while. They are interested in working as interns on a farm. The number of people looking for an internship is increasing. It's happening all over the world. A farming job fair in Japan attracted 1,400 people recently. In Colorado, a vegetable farmer named Rob Johnson received about 100 email inquiries for internships this year. He only got 15 two years ago. Farm internships are definitely becoming more popular. This syndrome benefits both the young interns and the older farmers who take them on.

Farm work has a lot of benefits for young people. They can get free rent and all the fresh air they want. Hard work improves their fitness, and waking up early every day teaches them a sense of responsibility. "Of course I won't be able to retire early. But I can hear the birds all day, and the view from my 'office' is fantastic," explains Sarah Thompson, pointing to the cornfields behind her. The 27-year-old from Seattle has been working at Johnson's farm for three years and says she wants to stay and learn all she can.

While farmers teach young people about farming, the young people introduce farmers to new technology. Farmers who have been running their farms the same way for many years can update their methods with the modern ideas their interns bring. Farmers can learn to use new technology for growing plants. **They** can learn updated ways to cultivate their crops. Furthermore, young interns can create websites for the farms. Farmers can post news about their harvests, and customers can ask about next season's fruits or vegetables.

Not so long ago, most people believed that working on farms was only for old people. Now times are changing. More and more young people are interested in farm work, and the number of internships is increasing. The experience has a lot of benefits for both young people and farmers. They cooperate and learn from each other.

Comprehension Check

A. True or False

*Check **True** or **False**.*

		True	False
1.	Working on a farm has always been popular.	☐	☐
2.	Fewer and fewer people want to find something to do on a farm.	☐	☐
3.	Interns have to pay rent when they live on a farm.	☐	☐
4.	Young workers can learn a sense of responsibility living on a farm.	☐	☐
5.	Sarah Thompson just started to work on a farm.	☐	☐
6.	Young people are also teaching farmers things about technology.	☐	☐
7.	Farmers are learning how to communicate better with their customers.	☐	☐
8.	Interns and farmers learn from their cooperation.	☐	☐

B. Complete the Passage

Fill in the blanks with the words in the box. Change the form of the words if necessary.

fantastic	benefit	internship	technology	cooperate

The number of farm **1.** ____________ is increasing. There are a lot of **2.** ____________ to being on a farm. For example, workers don't have to pay rent. The air is fresh and the view is **3.** ____________ too. There are benefits to farmers as well. They learn new **4.** ____________ and modern methods. Farmers and interns **5.** ____________ with each other and it's good for everyone.

C. Multiple Choice

Circle the answer.

1. What does **they** refer to in the third paragraph?
   - **a.** customers
   - **b.** farmers
   - **c.** interns
   - **d.** young people

2. Working on a farm includes all of the following benefits BUT ...
   - **a.** a great view.
   - **b.** clean and fresh air.
   - **c.** responsibilities for their works.
   - **d.** being paid well.

3. How do the young workers help the farmers?
   - **a.** They purchase all the vegetables.
   - **b.** They grow plants by themselves.
   - **c.** They introduce new technology.
   - **d.** They bring some air conditioners.

4. Which of the following is true?
   - **a.** The number of interns on a farm is increasing.
   - **b.** Interns and farmers don't get along well.
   - **c.** The young people don't work out for farmers.
   - **d.** Farmers want to live in cities.

UNIT 9 A World Undersea?

Have You Heard...?

Islands have been disappearing since the beginning of time. In 1613 B.C., a volcano exploded, breaking the Greek island of Santorini into pieces. The volcano also caused 100-meter-high waves. The explosion was heard in Sweden. In 1883, four volcanic explosions destroyed Indonesia's island of Krakatoa, killing 120,000 people. Bodies were still being washed up on Africa's beaches a year later.

Before We Read

A. Read and Answer

Tuvalu, a tiny state between Hawaii and Australia, is **calling for** the rest of the world to make every effort to fight global warming before it **sinks** into the ocean. Home to fewer than 11,000 **citizens**, the country is made up of nine small islands. At the **current** rate the sea is rising, it is **predicted** that Tuvalu will **disappear** in the next 30 to 50 years.

Replace the words in italics with the words in bold above. Change the form of the words if necessary.

1. The city is *asking* people to take public transportation.
   → ______________________________
2. The medicine won't make your pain *go away*, but it will make you feel better.
   → ______________________________
3. Josh Thompson is the *present* manager of the company.
   → ______________________________
4. Noriko is an American *national*, but she is originally from Japan.
   → ______________________________
5. The newspapers *guessed* that the president would win a second term.
   → ______________________________
6. The ship hit an iceberg in the Antarctic and began to *go down in the water* on Tuesday.
   → ______________________________

B. Make Predictions

Read the article on pages 92 and 93. Answer the questions.

1. Where will you probably see the article?
   - ☐ in an online journal
   - ☐ in the evening newspaper
   - ☐ at a government office in Hawaii
   - ☐ on a TV commercial
2. What is the topic of the text?
   - ☐ Tuvalu's culture
   - ☐ disappearing islands
   - ☐ the highest point in Tuvalu
   - ☐ the musical ability of Telito's family

C. Scan

Read the article again. Discuss the following questions with your partner.

1. What happened to Lohachara?
2. Where is Tuvalu?
3. What kind of lifestyle do Tuvaluans live?
4. What are some foods people in Tuvalu eat?

Sign In | Not a member? Register

World Traveler

Track 17

THE WORLD IS YOUR OYSTER

Destinations | Lifestyles | Travel | Cultures | Photography | Food & Drink

Here Today, Gone Tomorrow

World Traveler recently ran a story on Lohachara. This island used to be a part of India. Several years ago, swelling waters caused this island to disappear. At the time, 6,000 people lived there. All of these people lost their homes and property. Furthermore, they were forced to move.

Today, over one million people live on small islands like Lohachara worldwide. The citizens of these islands live under the threat of losing their homes, countries, and even their lives. *World Traveler* has received hundreds of emails from readers. We picked one letter that struck a chord and asked the writer to provide a picture of his country as well. We've shared his email here. Thanks for your support.

Sign In | Not a member? Register

World Traveler

THE WORLD IS YOUR OYSTER

Destinations | Lifestyles | Travel | Cultures | Photography | Food & Drink

Gilbert Telito(Funafuti, Tuvalu)

I wouldn't be surprised if you haven't heard of Tuvalu. It's at the end of the world, past Hawaii, out in the Pacific Ocean. The highest point on our islands is 4.5 meters. Plus Tuvalu is covered with sand, which washes out to sea all the time. We're already one of the smallest countries on earth, so we're not happy about how our islands are growing smaller.

Tuvaluans still live a traditional lifestyle. Each family does its part to contribute. We're given a task, the ***salanga***, to perform for the community we live in, such as fishing, farming, or maybe something like keeping the books or teaching. My family, a large and fun-loving group, is in charge of providing music at ceremonies.

Life in Tuvalu has never been easy. Since we only have sand for soil, we've always counted on fishing. We also have coconuts and taro, a tropical potato, which we plant under stones to keep the sand from blowing away. It's a simple life, but one we are used to. If we have to move, I don't know what we'll do to survive. We love our country. We want to stay where we are. And we want the world to start taking notice of Tuvalu.

Comprehension Check

A. Fill in the Missing Letters

Complete the sentences with the words from the article. Change the form of the words if necessary.

1. The homes and **p**__________ of the people living in Lohachara were destroyed by the ocean.
2. Tuvaluans are worried about **s**__________ waters like Lohachara.
3. The story about global warming **s**__________ a chord with Tuvaluan readers.
4. Tuvalu is **c**__________ with sand, and it washes out to sea.
5. The people of Tuvalu need to **c**__________ to the community.
6. Tuvaluans often play music at special **c**__________.
7. For food, Tuvaluans have **c**__________ on fishing. They also grow fruit like coconut and taro.
8. People in Tuvalu are worried what they'll do to **s**__________?

B. True or False

*Check **True** or **False**.*

	True	False
1. The website had a story about an island that is still in India.	☐	☐
2. More than 1,000,000 people live on small islands like the one in India.	☐	☐
3. Almost nobody has written to *World Traveler* about its story.	☐	☐
4. *World Traveler* has put a picture of Tuvalu on its website.	☐	☐
5. Tuvalu has high mountains and valleys.	☐	☐
6. People in Tuvalu keep a traditional lifestyle still now.	☐	☐
7. In Tuvalu, coconuts and taro are planted under stones.	☐	☐
8. Telito hopes his story will strike a chord with people around the world.	☐	☐

C. Vocabulary Building

Circle the synonym of the word/phrase in bold.

1. In spring, ice melts and the water flows into the **swelling** rivers.
   a. growing **b.** shrinking
2. My uncle left me some **property** in London when he passed away.
   a. time **b.** assets
3. You're late to work **all the time**. In the future, try to come earlier.
   a. regularly **b.** never
4. Johnson won't be able to **perform** his usual duties. He has a broken hand.
   a. find out **b.** carry out
5. Don't worry, Preston. We can **count on** Jerome to do a good job.
   a. depend on **b.** search out
6. Doug is from Africa. He's not **used to** cold weather.
   a. accustomed to **b.** known for
7. This is important. Please **take notice of** what I'm going to tell you.
   a. study up on **b.** pay attention to

D. Complete the Sentences

Fill in the blanks with the words in the box. Change the form of the words if necessary.

1. | used to | be used to |
   |---|---|

- Hansa comes from Thailand, so she ____________ spicy food.
- My father ____________ smoke a lot. Thankfully, he quit a few years ago.

2. | furthermore | in addition to |
   |---|---|

- ____________ eating out, we're going to see a movie.
- There are some snacks on the table; ____________, we have tea and coffee.

3. | as well | also | either |
   |---|---|---|

- Scott doesn't like daytime TV shows and Ed doesn't ____________.
- We're going to the beach. Why don't you come along ____________?
- Alisa dances beautifully. She ____________ plays the violin and piano.

E. Multiple Choice

Circle the answer.

1. What is true about Lohachara Island?
   a. It now belongs to another country.
   b. It disappeared under the water.
   c. It has started to vanish recently.
   d. People in Lohachara will be moving soon.

2. Over million people are under the threat of ...
   a. keeping their tradition.
   b. moving to a new house.
   c. losing their nations.
   d. performing for the community.

3. Where is Tuvalu?
   a. in Hawaii
   b. at the end of the country
   c. in the Pacific Ocean
   d. a part of India

4. What does ***salanga*** mean in the letter?
   a. the community
   b. a festival
   c. a kind of music
   d. a job

5. Why do Tuvaluans plant taro under stones?
   a. The stones are too heavy to move.
   b. It is the simplest way of farming.
   c. The sand will blow away if there are no stones.
   d. Stones are the only thing they have.

Vocabulary Check

A. Fill in the Missing Letters

Complete the sentences with the words from the article.

1. The Empire State Building is one of the main tourist **d**__________ in New York. (where you're going)
2. After the typhoon, we couldn't cross the **s**__________ river. (rising)
3. We are not responsible for any damage to your personal **p**__________. (the things you own)
4. Rubin was fired because he was not able to **p**__________ his duties. (do)
5. I watched the opening **c**__________ of the Olympic Games on TV. (an important event)

B. Words with Different Meanings

Match the word in bold with its definition.

1
My aunt **runs** a restaurant in London. _____
A local newspaper **ran** her story. _____
Definition: **a** *v.* to manage **b** *v.* to print or broadcast something

2
It's everyone's job to save the **earth**. _____
The **earth** here isn't good for farming. _____
Definition: **a** *n.* planet **b** *n.* soil

3
Valerie always tries to help people. She says it feels good to **contribute**. _____
There are three writers **contributing** to the book. _____
Definition: **a** *v.* to write articles **b** *v.* to be helpful

C. Meanings in Context

Choose the meaning of the phrase in bold.

1. If you get a good education, **the world is your oyster**.
   a. The future will be great.
   b. The future will be scary.

2. Your speech on what we can do to clean up our world **struck a chord with** me.
   a. was agreed upon by
   b. was protested by

3. Who's going to **keep the books** at our new restaurant?
   a. go to the library
   b. do the accounting

4. You'll have to talk to Mr. Ramirez. He's **in charge of** this department.
   a. the head of
   b. the secretary of

Reading Strategy

Appositives

TIP

An appositive often helps us understand more about the word or phrase it follows. Sometimes, the words before the appositive explain new vocabulary in it.

- The tacos, **a kind of Mexican food made with tortillas and meat**, are really good at this restaurant.
- Tuvaluans are given a task, **the *salanga***, to perform for the community they live in.

• Give It a Try •

PART I

We often place commas around an appositive. Add commas to the following sentences.

1. The car a 1989 Toyota was badly damaged.
2. On Venus the closest planet to the Earth there is no water.
3. Telito's family a friendly bunch of people has to play music at the islands' ceremonies.
4. People living in this country eat taro a kind of purple potato that they plant below rocks and drink *kao*.

PART II

Combine the following sentences with appositives.

1. Henry lives in Japan. He is an American.
   → ____________________
2. Poland is a country between Germany and Russia. It has many beautiful old towns.
   → ____________________
3. *Kao* tastes delicious. It is a warm, alcoholic drink.
   → ____________________
4. The HSR is very convenient. HSR stands for High Speed Rail.
   → ____________________

Further Reading

Fighting Mother Nature for Land

Track 18

Much has been written about global warming, especially how it is influencing ocean levels. Islands around the world are vanishing, and coasts are falling into the water. But people aren't entirely at the mercy of Mother Nature. In fact, we have been stealing land from the ocean for thousands of years. It's a continuing battle, one that is not going to end anytime soon.

One way people have been able to take land back is by using dikes.* These are like walls, but made from dirt. A successful example is in the Netherlands. A fifth of the country's land is carved out of the ocean. That's 7,000 square kilometers. Big parts of downtown Hong Kong and Singapore also sit on areas that were once underwater. And Mexico City, the largest city in the world, is built on an ancient lake. It was filled in with earth and the bones of people a long time ago.

The idea of land reclamation* isn't new. The Roman writer Tacitus wrote about dikes in Germany 2,000 years ago. The Germans actually destroyed their dikes to slow Roman soldiers. In 1250, a 126-kilometer-long wall, called the *Westfriese Omringdijk*, was completed in the Netherlands. Americans have also been building them in cities such as Boston and New Orleans ever since the 17th century.

It will be interesting to see how the world responds to global warming. Is it possible that some of the small islands under threat can be saved by dikes or another kind of technology? The people of Maldives, for example, are building **themselves** a new, flood-resistant island. Some, however, say looking for technological solutions is wrong. We need to change how we view the planet — and our bad habits. Others think we have technology to make life easier, so let's use it. Perhaps both sides are right. This discussion will grow louder every time the sea claims a new place.

Reference:

* **dike** *a wall built to keep back water*
* **reclamation** *getting something back*

Comprehension Check

A. Main Idea

Write the number of the paragraph to match each topic.

1. People have been taking back land from the ocean for a long time. ______
2. People are looking more closely at the battle between humans and nature. ______
3. What are we going to do about global warming in the future? ______
4. It is possible to protect land from the ocean by building walls made from dirt. ______

B. Summary

Choose the answer.

Global warming is influencing ocean levels. Islands are now 1. ____________ because ocean waters are rising. But there is something we can do, and people have been doing for a long time — build 2. ____________ to keep the ocean back. Some of the more successful examples of land 3. ____________ have taken place in the Netherlands. About 20 percent of this country is reclaimed from the ocean. It also has a 126-kilometer- 4. ____________ dike, called the *Westfriese Omringdijk*. Built in 1250, it is the largest of its kind. With more and more islands coming 5. ____________ threat, it'll be interesting to see how the world responds.

1. **a.** vanishing	**b.** replying	**c.** curving	**d.** foreseeing
2. **a.** islands	**b.** bridges	**c.** boats	**d.** dikes
3. **a.** reclaims	**b.** reclaiming	**c.** reclamation	**d.** reclaimers
4. **a.** long	**b.** longer	**c.** longest	**d.** too long
5. **a.** inside	**b.** under	**c.** over	**d.** around

C. Multiple Choice

Circle the answer.

1. Which of the following is true?
   a. We can't do anything to fight nature.
   b. We have never been at the mercy of nature.
   c. We can do something about lost land.
   d. We've always been afraid of the ocean.

2. Dikes are all of the following BUT ...
   a. walls made from dirt.
   b. near the ocean.
   c. a successful example in Netherlands.
   d. a cause of flooding.

3. How has Mexico City changed since ancient times?
   a. The city has been sinking.
   b. A lake has disappeared.
   c. It has a long dike.
   d. It's not so big now.

4. What does **themselves** refer to in the last paragraph?
   a. small islands
   b. dikes
   c. citizens
   d. discussions

UNIT 10

Fashion over Time

Have You Heard...?

People will pay a lot of money for a piece of fashion history. On May 25th, 2001, a Levi Strauss & Co. employee bought a 100-year-old pair of Levi's for $46,532. The jeans had been found in a Nevada mining town. The company later made 500 copies of the jeans and sold them for $300 each. Years later, in 2008, another pair that was more than 100 years old was found inside a California gold mine. It was later sold online for $36,099.

Before We Read

A. Read and Answer

Levi Strauss, the inventor of blue jeans, arrived in San Francisco in 1853 looking for big money. It was the high point of the California Gold **Rush**. Strauss, a German **immigrant**, got rich by selling goods to the miners of California. At the time, laborers often complained that their pants were easily **torn**. So Strauss started making **durable** pants with **denim** and **copper**. Blue jeans soon became the **uniform** for miners and other workers. Today, jeans are a **symbol** of American culture.

Write the words in bold above in the appropriate space. Change the form of the words if necessary.

	Word	Definition
1		a type of cloth used to make jeans
2		someone who moves into a new country
3		a situation in which lots of people suddenly try to do something
4		damaged; ripped
5		a thing that represents something else
6		clothing worn by all the members of a group
7		can be used for a long time
8		a soft brown metal

TIP
Words that end in –**or** *and* –**er** *usually refer to someone who does a particular job.*
Read the passage again. Circle the –**or** *and* –**er** *words you see and discuss their meanings with your partner.*

B. Make Predictions

Read the title and the first paragraph on page 102. What do you think the reading is about?

- ☐ fashion in the 1500s
- ☐ the American clothing industry
- ☐ new fashion trends
- ☐ the history of jeans

C. Scan

Read the article on pages 102 and 103. What do the following numbers refer to?

a. pairs of jeans the average American owns
b. millions of dollars Americans spend on jeans each year
c. how much a pair of jeans cost in the late 1800s
d. when jeans started to become high fashion
e. when the California Gold Rush happened

1. 14 _____ **2.** 7 _____ **3.** 1848 _____ **4.** 1.50 _____ **5.** 1980 _____

A Piece of History in Your Closet

Track 19

Jeans. Good luck finding a closet without a pair of them. Jeans are so fashionable that people in the U.S. spend about $14 million on them each year. The average American owns seven pairs. It's not a new fashion trend though. The material for jeans dates back to the 1500s.

Jeans are made from a fabric* called denim, or *de Nîmes* in French. The strong, blue material was made in the French city of Nîmes. The word jeans is related to the Italian sailors who wore them. The sailors came from Genoa and were called Genoese, which sounds like jeans.

Jeans were changed by the California Gold Rush of 1848. A German immigrant named Levi Strauss started making denim jeans with copper to make the pockets stronger. Strauss sold his jeans to the gold miners, and jeans were soon the uniform for laborers. Jeans especially became a symbol for cowboys. In the late 1800s, a pair of jeans cost $1.50.

By the 1940s, people were wearing jeans for leisure. In the 1950s, stars like Elvis Presley and Marlon Brando made jeans popular with teenagers. Jeans also became associated with James Dean and young rebels. Schools, movie theaters, and restaurants even banned **them**.

During the 1960s and '70s, hippies changed the style of jeans. The bottoms went from being straight to being bell-shaped. Hippies decorated their denim with flowers and peace designs.

Jeans entered the world of high fashion in the 1980s. Designers sold jeans that were already torn and dyed in different colors. The bell-bottoms* of the 1970s were out, and skinny jeans were in. The material wasn't just used for pants anymore either. Denim jackets, purses, shoes, and even furniture became popular.

Today, you can find jeans in any shape or color. You can also wear a pair just about anywhere you go. Jeans are truly an icon.

Reference:

* **fabric** *material*
* **bell-bottoms** *pants with wide bottoms*

People Who Changed Jeans

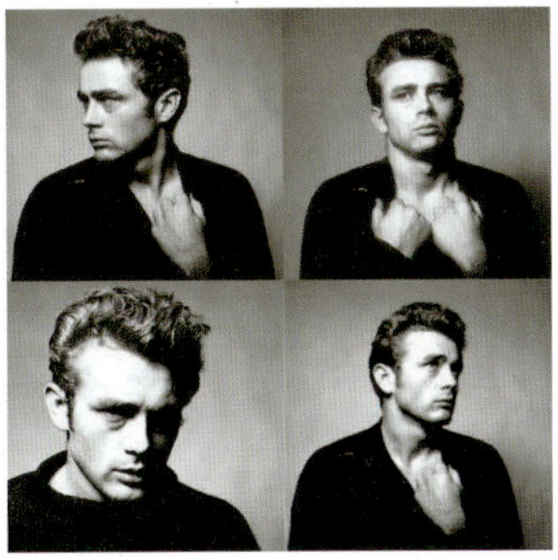

James Dean is famous for his role in the 1955 film *Rebel without a Cause*. Dean plays a teenager who doesn't agree with his parents. Many teenagers thought Dean was cool and copied the way he dressed. Dean once said, "Dream as if you'll live forever. Live as if you'll die today." These words represent his style.

Hippie culture started in the 1960s in America. Hippies were teenagers and young adults who valued peace and love. They were against war and didn't like their government. Many grew long hair and wore unusual clothes.

Comprehension Check

A. Put in Order

Put the following events in order.

- a. Jeans were high fashion and started to appear on runways.
- b. The material for jeans was made for the first time in the French city.
- c. Many people moved west as the gold rush began in California.
- d. People began wearing jeans for leisure, not just labor.
- e. Jeans became popular among teenagers after movie stars started wearing them.
- f. Hippies decorated their jeans with flowers and peace signs.
- g. Jeans became a symbol for cowboys in the western part of the U.S.

_____ → _____ → _____ → _____ → _____ → _____ → _____

B. Fill in the Missing Letters

Complete the sentences with the words from the article. Change the form of the words if necessary.

1. The origin of the word denim is **r**__________ to the name of Nîmes, a city in France.
2. The word jeans came from the hometown of the Italian **s**__________ who wore them.
3. Jeans were first created as work pants for gold **m**__________ during the Gold Rush in California.
4. In 1848, denim contained **c**__________ which made the pockets stronger.
5. People **a**__________ jeans with rebels, so there was once a **b**__________ on jeans in some schools and restaurants.
6. The hippies of the 1960s and 1970s **b**__________ jeans with flowers.
7. People started to wear **s**__________ jeans in the 1980s.
8. Designer companies introduced **t**__________ and **d**__________ jeans to the public in 1980s.

C. True or False

Check ***True*** *or* ***False****.*

		True	False
1.	The word for the fabric of jeans came from the name of a town in Italy.	☐	☐
2.	People had begun wearing jeans for leisure by the 1940s.	☐	☐
3.	An immigrant from Germany sold jeans to students as their uniform.	☐	☐
4.	Furniture that was made out of denim became popular in the 1980s.	☐	☐
5.	The 1950s were when people were first allowed to wear jeans in movie theaters and restaurants.	☐	☐
6.	Hippies wore skinny, straight jeans with flowers and peace designs on them.	☐	☐
7.	In 1980S, designers made clothes and accessories with denim.	☐	☐

D. Vocabulary Building

Circle the synonym of the word in bold.

1. The shirt was made of high-quality **material**.
   a. jeans **b.** fabric
2. My cell phone is **strong**. I have dropped it many times, but it still works.
   a. durable **b.** fragile
3. People are **banned** from smoking on airplanes.
   a. permitted **b.** prohibited
4. I've noticed that bright clothing is **in** this year.
   a. fashionable **b.** strange
5. Many people wore bell-bottoms before, but now they are **out**.
   a. trendy **b.** old-fashioned
6. I can't fit in these **skinny** jeans. Do you have bigger ones?
   a. loose **b.** narrow

Circle the antonym of the word/phrase in bold.

1. James thinks Tracy **spent** too much money on her car.
   a. lent **b.** saved
2. For most people, weekends are a time for **leisure**.
   a. work **b.** relaxation
3. Years ago, flip-flops were cheap shoes for the beach, but today they are **high fashion**.
   a. fancy **b.** out of style
4. My pants are **torn** because my dog chewed them.
   a. in good condition **b.** heavily damaged

E. Multiple Choice

Circle the answer.

1. Who did NOT wear jeans in the 1800s?
   a. miners
   b. cowboys
   c. laborers
   d. designers

2. Who did NOT make jeans popular in the 1950s?
   a. Levi Strauss
   b. Marlon Brando
   c. Elvis Presley
   d. James Dean

3. What does **them** refer to in the fourth paragraph?
   a. movie stars
   b. jeans
   c. teenagers
   d. stars

4. Which denim product is NOT mentioned?
   a. shoes
   b. scarf
   c. purses
   d. jackets

Vocabulary Check

A. Fill in the Missing Letters

Complete the sentences with the words from the article.

1. The current **t**____________ is towards hiring more part-time workers. (likely to do something)
2. My friend Clint is a **c**____________. He lives in Texas and works on a farm. (a person who cares for cattle)
3. Riding a bike is my favorite **l**____________ activity. (time when you can relax)
4. She likes to wear **s**____________ pants to show the shape of her legs. (very tight)
5. Some say John Lennon was an **i**____________ for hippies. (something that represents an important idea)

B. Meanings in Context

Choose the meaning of the word/phrase in bold.

1. The **average** family in that city owns two or more cars.
   a. every
   b. typical

2. The Chinese poem **dates back to** 1320 A.D.
   a. starts from
   b. stops in

3. The doctor said my memory loss **was related to** the accident.
   a. was separated from
   b. was connected to

4. Many people **associate** ice cream **with** childhood.
   a. link ... with
   b. confuse ... with

5. The famous singer is interested in **high fashion**.
   a. the traditional style
   b. the newest style

C. Complete the Sentences

Fill in the blanks with the words in the box. Change the form of the words if necessary.

rush	dye	rebel	ban	tear

1. Smoking is ____________ in public places like restaurants and hospitals.
2. My hair is naturally black, but I ____________ it brown.
3. I threw the jacket away. It's old and ____________.
4. Many people thought Elvis was a ____________. He didn't do what other people told him to.
5. After they found oil in Pennsylvania in the 1870s, there was a big oil ____________.

Reading Strategy

Understanding Time Order

TIP 1

Do you remember the time adverbs from Unit 3? Write down those clue words in the box.

TIP 2

We'll be looking at some common time prepositions: in, on, at, by, during, for, and until. They are usually followed by nouns.

• Give It a Try •

PART I

*Use the prepositions from **TIP2** to fill in the blanks. Write X if no preposition is needed.*

1. This style was popular ______________ the 1970s.
2. I heard the noise ______________ 10:30 last night.
3. We bought the company ______________ Thursday, May 22nd.
4. I went shopping with my sister ______________ last Tuesday.
5. I need to finish this report ______________ tomorrow morning
6. ______________ my time in London, I visited a lot of interesting places.
7. The concert went ______________ 11 o'clock.
8. I was waiting for him ______________ two hours.

PART II

Complete the passage with the words in the box. Change the form of the words if necessary.

when	date back to	in	later	previously	in the beginning

The soft drink Coca-Cola **1.** ______________ the late 1800s. It was invented in 1886 by John Pemberton, a pharmacist from Georgia. **2.** ______________, Pemberton made a drink called French Wine of Coca, which included wine, cocaine, and caffeine. **3.** ______________ the government made alcohol illegal, Pemberton took out the wine and added kola nut to make Coca-Cola. The drink got its name from the cocaine and kola nut in it. Cocaine was taken out of the recipe **4.** ______________ 1905, but kola nut is still used today. **5.** ______________, only nine drinks were sold per day. Total sales were $50 in the first year. Just nine years **6.** ______________, Coca-Cola was drunk in every state in America. Now more than a billion drinks are sold each day all over the world.

Further Reading

Fashion Timeline

Track 20

1930s People had less money during the Great Depression, so clothes became practical and conservative. Women's hair and skirts were longer again. As the Depression ended, men were asking for new pinstripe* suits and women wore evening gowns. Even gangsters influenced fashion, making suits more dramatic.

1940s The restriction of goods during World War II included clothing, so fancy clothing was seen as a waste. It was considered patriotic to fix clothes at home.

1950s For the first time, teenagers had a voice in fashion. Nice young men wore sweaters and wool pants; bad boys wore leather jackets and jeans. Young women wore either wide poodle skirts or tight pencil skirts.

1960s The Vietnam War inspired the hippie movement. Long straight hair and peace signs were popular. The ease of traveling introduced Eastern fashion into Western styles. The miniskirt was invented, and bell-bottom jeans were also fashionable. Men styled their hair like the Beatles.

1970s This decade is remembered for its disco style: hot pants and cat suits, bell-bottoms, and platform shoes — for women and men.

1980s Women dressed more like men to get ahead at work. Fashion was exaggerated with big hair, big sunglasses, and big shoulder pads. Men's casual wear was a white suit jacket, a colored T-shirt, and jeans.

1990s Fashion changed again. Grunge, a dirty-looking style, was popular. Comfort became more important than style, and black filled everyone's closet.

2000s Hoodies,* trucker hats, and baggy clothes — oh my! Young men wore T-shirts with tattoo-style images. Girls paired miniskirts with Ugg boots. Skinny jeans, which first came out in the '50s, came back skinnier than ever.

2010s Loose pants, baggy jeans, and comfortable clothing are in. We can see designer jogging suits and sweat pants as well as colorful shorts, high dresses, and big glasses. Men and women are fashionable and comfortable at the same time.

The future Fashion of the future shows a trend towards unisex. We predict men and women alike will wear long shorts, utility pants, tight shirts, and sandals. Hats will be in. Colorful clothes will go out of fashion. Gray, brown, black, and white clothes will be in. Are you ready?

Reference:

* **pinstripe** *a thin line on a fabric*
* **hoodie** *a sweatshirt with a hood*

Comprehension Check

A. Classification

Match the sentence with the matching decade.

1. A dirty-looking style of clothing became popular. ____________
2. Criminals affected the fashion trends. ____________
3. Many girls wore miniskirts and Ugg boots. ____________
4. The hippie movement had a big impact on fashion. ____________
5. Disco was the hot fashion. ____________
6. Many people fixed their own clothes in order to help their country. ____________

B. Match

Match the picture with the name of it.

a
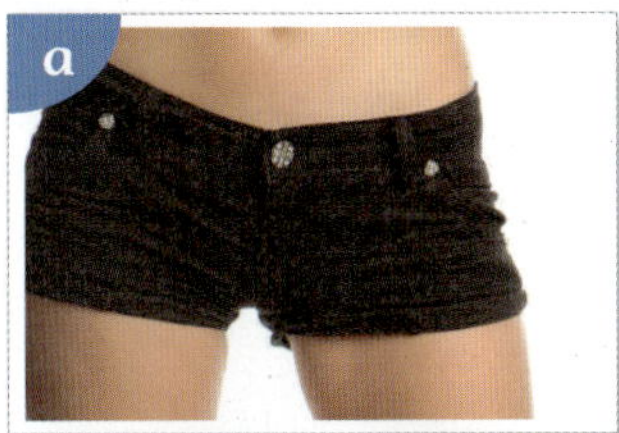

b

c

d

e

f

1. hot pants ______
2. pinstripe suit ______
3. platform shoes ______
4. bell-bottoms ______
5. trucker hat ______
6. Ugg boots ______

C. Multiple Choice

Circle the answer.

1. In the 1950s, what did bad boys wear?
   a. poodle skirts and T-shirts
   b. sweaters and wool pants
   c. pinstripe suits and hats
   d. leather jackets and jeans

2. According to the reading, what was the reason the hippie movement started?
   a. Great Depression
   b. the Vietnam War
   c. disco
   d. World War II

3. When was the miniskirt invented?
   a. in the 1990s
   b. in the 2000s
   c. in the 1960s
   d. in the 1970s

4. When did skinny jeans come back into style?
   a. in the 2000s
   b. in the 1930s
   c. in the 1950s
   d. in the 1970s

UNIT 11

The Oldest Buildings on Earth

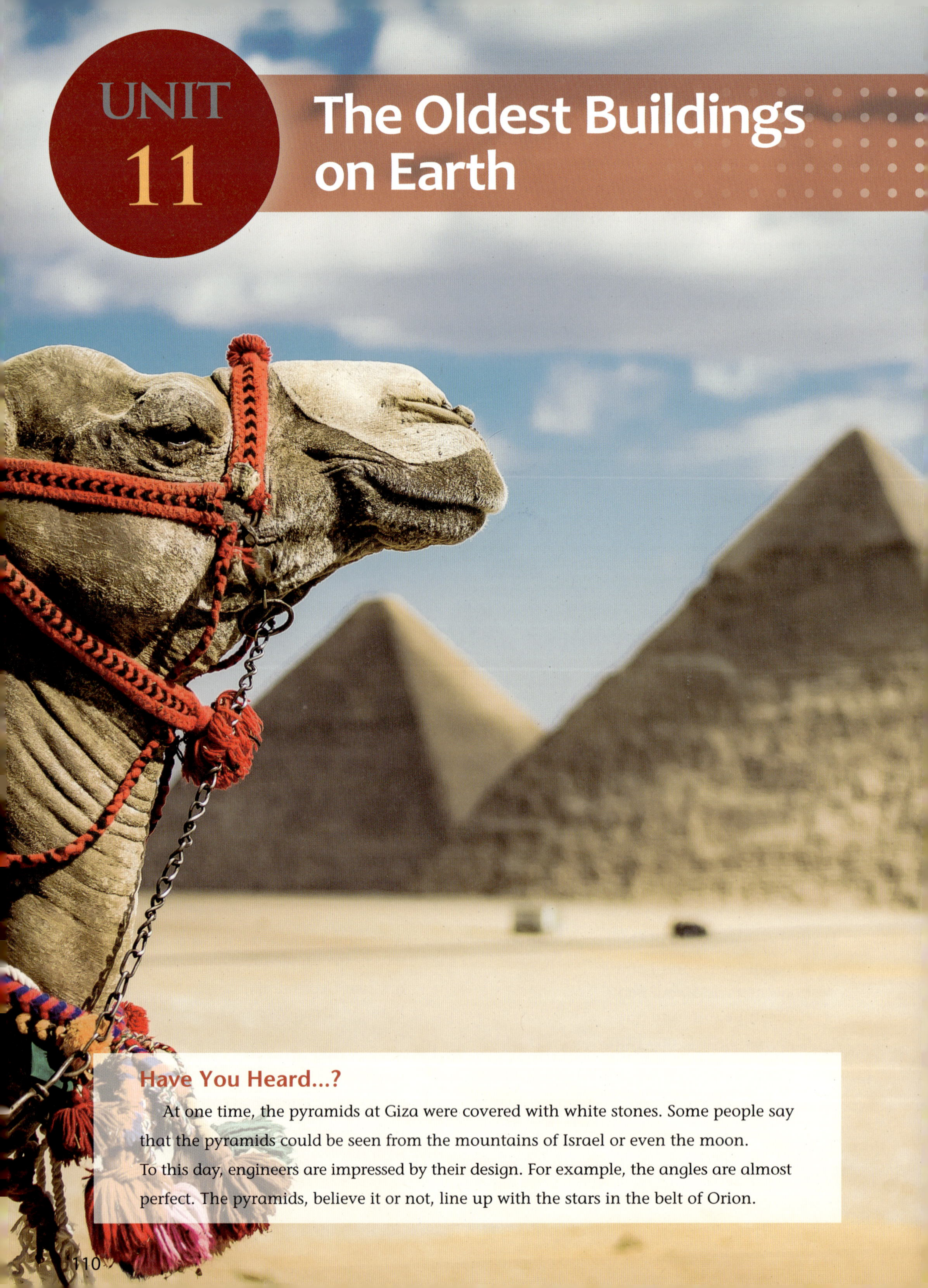

Have You Heard...?

At one time, the pyramids at Giza were covered with white stones. Some people say that the pyramids could be seen from the mountains of Israel or even the moon. To this day, engineers are impressed by their design. For example, the angles are almost perfect. The pyramids, believe it or not, line up with the stars in the belt of Orion.

Before We Read

A. Read and Answer

The Great Pyramid of Khufu is the oldest and largest of the three pyramids at Giza. It is made of more than two million blocks of stone. Each stone **weighs** about 2,200 kilograms. This **impressive** structure was built for the Pharaoh Khufu as a **tomb**. It is said it took 20 years to build the pyramid and the construction finished in around 2560 B.C. It is the only one of the famous Seven Wonders of the Ancient World that still stands. How the pyramid was built is still a **mystery**.

Write the words in bold above in the appropriate space. Change the form of the words if necessary.

	Word	Definition
1		amazing
2		a place where a dead person is buried
3		something people do not understand
4		to have a certain weight

B. Main Idea

Read the article on pages 112 and 113. Match the sentence with the paragraph.

1. We know what was done with the pharaoh's body after he died. ______
3. Sometimes we should just enjoy how special the pyramids are. ______
3. The size of the pyramids is impressive. ______
4. Nobody is sure how the pyramids were built. ______
5. It took a long time to build the pyramids. ______

TIP
Look for the main idea in the first or last sentence of each paragraph. Skimming through the paragraph will also help you to understand.

C. Scan

Read the article again. What do the following numbers refer to?

a. the number of years it took to build a pyramid
b. the number of pyramid workers
c. the weight in kilograms of each block in the pyramids
d. when the Eiffel Tower was built

1. 1889 ______ **2.** 2,200 ______ **3.** 30,000 ______ **4.** 20 ______

Exploring the Pyramids of Egypt

Track 21

The pyramids of Egypt have always been a mystery. Who built them? Were they really tombs? Were they filled with mummies* and treasure? What other functions did they serve? Even the ancient Greeks and Romans could not answer these questions. They just knew that the pyramids had stood for ages.

Although we still don't know all the answers, there is one thing that we do know: the pyramid was the pharaoh's tomb. After he died, the pharaoh was turned into a mummy. He was then placed inside the pyramid with his gold, religious items, records of the past, and other treasures. The Egyptians believed that without a body, the spirit of the pharaoh would wander aimlessly forever.

Of course, mummies and treasure aren't the only things that make the pyramids interesting. What about their size? Until the Eiffel Tower was built in 1889, the Great Pyramid of Khufu was the tallest building in the world. It was built with over two million blocks, weighing 2,200 kilograms each! 30,000 people worked ten hours a day for 20 years to complete its construction. Some people think these workers were slaves from other countries. Others believe that at least some of the builders were skilled workers who were paid for their time and labor.

The construction of the pyramids is even more impressive. To begin with, the blocks were pulled over a few kilometers. Then, they were pushed up ramps* by workers. Historians believe the Egyptians didn't have wheels to help them. They didn't have iron tools to work with either. All of this took place under the hot desert sun, day in and day out, for around 20 years. That's how long it took to build just one pyramid!

Information like this makes people wonder how the pyramids were built without using machines. Although we know more about the pyramids than before, some things will always be a mystery. Sometimes, it's nice just to appreciate the beauty of these great structures.

Reference:

* **mummy** *a dead body that is covered in cloth*
* **ramp** *a slope*

Comprehension Check

A. Short Answers

Write the answer.

1. Q: What items were put into the pyramids with the pharaohs?
   A: ______________________________.
2. Q: Why did the Egyptians turn their pharaohs into mummies?
   A: ______________________________.
3. Q: Who were probably paid for building the pyramids?
   A: ______________________________.
4. Q: How long did it take to build a pyramid?
   A: ______________________________.

B. True or False

*Check **True** or **False**.*

		True	False
1.	We know exactly who built the pyramids.	☐	☐
2.	The pyramids were built as tombs for the pharaohs.	☐	☐
3.	The Egyptians only put the pharaohs in the tombs — nothing else.	☐	☐
4.	The Great Pyramid of Khufu was built with stones.	☐	☐
5.	Everyone believes the pyramids were built by people who weren't paid.	☐	☐
6.	There were no wheels in Egypt at the time the pyramids were built.	☐	☐
7.	People assume some workers who built the pyramids were professionals.	☐	☐
8.	People only worked during the day on the pyramids.	☐	☐

C. Reference Word

Choose what the word in bold refers to.

1. **They** just knew that the ... stood for ages. (Paragraph 1)
   a. all of the years　　**b.** the pyramids
   c. the ancient Greeks and Romans　　**d.** the mummies and treasure
2. After **he** died, the pharaoh ... a mummy. (Paragraph 2)
   a. the mummy　　**b.** the pharaoh
   c. the gold　　**d.** the tomb
3. **It** was built with over two million blocks. (Paragraph 3)
   a. the Eiffel Tower　　**b.** a group of 30,000 workers
   c. the Great Pyramid of Khufu　　**d.** the food for the slaves
4. Then, **they** were pushed ... by workers. (Paragraph 4)
   a. the tallest buildings in the world　　**b.** the skilled workers
   c. the people from other countries　　**d.** the blocks used in pyramids

D. Vocabulary Building

Circle the synonym of the word in bold.

1. There is no historical **record** of the first spoken language.
   a. result b. account
2. The woman did hard manual **labor** in prison every day.
   a. understanding b. work
3. We visited the desert on our **impressive** tour of the city.
   a. weird b. awesome
4. The cabin by the lake is a two-story wooden **structure**.
   a. building b. level

Circle the antonym of the word in bold.

1. The police never solved the **mystery** of the man's death.
   a. fact b. joke
2. Since the email was invented, written letters have become a thing of the **past**.
   a. future b. route
3. The man had nothing to do, so he walked **aimlessly** around the city.
   a. sadly b. purposefully
4. Your old coin collection could be a **treasure** to some people.
   a. gold b. trash

E. Multiple Choice

Circle the answer.

1. Which of the following is true?
   a. We know who built the pyramids and how much treasure they had.
   b. We are unsure who built the pyramids and other functions they served.
   c. We do not know if the Greeks and Romans could answer our questions.
   d. We are uncertain if the pyramids have stood for a long time.

2. All of the following were put in the tombs BUT ...
   a. information about what happened before.
   b. things that were very valuable at the time.
   c. blocks that weighed over 2,200 kilograms each.
   d. things that had a religious meaning at one time.

3. What is NOT true about the Great Pyramid of Khufu?
   a. More than 2,000,000 blocks were used.
   b. It took 20 years to complete the construction.
   c. Builders were all slaves, so they didn't get paid.
   d. It was the tallest building before the Eiffel Tower was built.

4. Where did the blocks used for building the pyramids come from?
   a. the ground right below the pyramids
   b. from many other countries
   c. from a place a short distance away
   d. from a big mountain

Vocabulary Check

A. Fill in the Missing Letters

Complete the sentences with the words from the article.

1. In the 1400s, the Chinese **e**__________ the world with big ships. (travel around)
2. The **f**__________ of the basket is to carry fruit. (purpose)
3. The **r**__________ symbols in this church are very old. (about gods)
4. Although he is dead, we can feel his **s**__________ is with us. (soul)
5. Walt **w**__________ for years around Asia. Then he returned to New York and became a famous writer. (travel)
6. President Abraham Lincoln freed the **s**__________ in 1863. (someone owned by another person)
7. Usually **s**__________ workers make more money. (with experience)
8. People living in Napa Valley really **a**__________ fine wine. (enjoy)

B. Meanings in Context

Choose the meaning of the phrase in bold.

1. Karen and I have known each other **for ages**.
   a. for a short time
   b. for a long time

2. It will take you **at least 20 minutes** to get to the train station.
   a. 20 minutes or more
   b. less than 20 minutes

3. The wedding will **take place** in Sydney.
   a. be cancelled
   b. be held

4. My brother plays computer games **day in and day out**.
   a. during daytime
   b. all the time

C. Words with Different Meanings

Match the word in bold with its definition.

1. Danny's old furniture is his greatest **treasure**. _____
   I **treasure** the ring my mother gave me. _____
   Definition: ⓐ *v.* to keep something that is valuable ⓑ *n.* a valuable thing

2. A big truck is **blocking** the road. _____
   We kept the food cold with a large **block** of ice. _____
   Definition: ⓐ *v.* to prevent anything from going through ⓑ *n.* a piece of hard material

3. The construction of the library is expected to be **complete** in February. _____
   The novel took three years to **complete**. _____
   Definition: ⓐ *v.* to finish doing something ⓑ *adj.* finished

Reading Strategy

Making Inferences and Drawing Conclusions

TIP

When we make inferences and draw conclusions, we understand details that are not in an article. Do this by focusing on the information the writer includes in the passage.

• Give It a Try •

PART I

Match the sentence with its inference.

- **a.** People have never really understood them.
- **b.** The pyramids must be very well built.
- **c.** The Egyptians believed that spirits should have somewhere to go.

1. The pyramids of Egypt have always been a mystery. ______
2. The Egyptians believed that without a body, the spirit of the pharaoh would wander aimlessly forever. ______
3. 30,000 people worked ten hours a day for 20 years to complete its construction. ______

PART II

Discuss with your partner what you can infer from the passage.

Every time I go to history class, I feel sleepy. I know that I shouldn't sleep in class, but I just can't help it. Miss Goulet gets angry when I fall asleep. Sometimes, she even shouts at me. But this doesn't worry me very much. Even when I don't sleep, she still doesn't look happy. I like math class better because I don't have to remember dates. What I want to do is become a math teacher. I want to teach other people what I know. I think I can make a difference in people's lives.

What I Read	Miss Goulet shouts at her students.
What I Know Already	People who shout look angry and are not liked by others.
What I Infer	The writer doesn't like his history teacher.

Further Reading

The Buildings History Left Behind

Track 22

Of the Seven Wonders of the Ancient World, only one remains: Egypt's pyramids. They have been able to stand the test of time. Do you know the Seven Wonders of the Modern World then? Some of them were actually built long ago.

Chichen Itza Pyramid, Mexico

After the pyramids in Egypt, this is the world's oldest pyramid. It was built by the Mayans, an ancient culture of Mexico.

Machu Picchu, Peru

Built on the top of a mountain, Machu Picchu was the highest town in the Incan world.

Nobody knows how the stones for Machu Picchu got there. The Incas had neither strong animals nor wheels to carry them.

Petra, Jordan

Petra is a cave, or many caves, carved into Mount Hor. The most famous structure at Petra is the treasury.* At one time, it was full of gold and silver.

Christ the Redeemer, Brazil

Overlooking the coast, this statue, a carving of Jesus, can be seen by all below. People come from all over the world to see it.

The Colosseum, Italy

The Colosseum is in the middle of downtown Rome. 2000 years ago, it was used for gladiatorial* games. It's a place everyone interested in history should visit. It has even been the location of an Oscar winning movie!

The Great Wall, China

The Great Wall of China was built 2,200 years ago to stop people from entering China. Four million people visit the Great Wall every year.

Taj Mahal, India

The Taj Mahal, with its cool white marble, is often called the most beautiful building in the world. It's beautiful for another reason too. The emperor of India had it built for his favorite wife after she died.

Which of these wonders have you visited? You don't need to love history in order to enjoy these attractions. **They** are something you'll never forget seeing.

Reference:

* **treasury** *a place where money or valuable things are kept*
* **gladiatorial** *related to fighting in ancient Rome*

Comprehension Check

A. Classification

Match the sentence with its attraction.

a. Chichen Itza Pyramid
b. Machu Picchu
c. Petra
d. Christ the Redeemer
e. The Colosseum
f. The Great Wall
g. Taj Mahal

1. This place was once used for saving treasure. ______
2. Only Egypt has older examples of this kind of structure. ______
3. This statue has a religious importance. ______
4. At one time, this place was used for fighting. ______
5. We are unsure of how this was built. ______
6. A long time ago, this was used to keep enemies out. ______
7. The ruler built this building to remember his wife. ______

B. Summary

Choose the answer.

Only one of the Seven Wonders of the Ancient World 1. ____________ : the Great Pyramid of Giza. The 2. ____________ world has its own list of wonders. It includes a pyramid in Mexico, a statue in Brazil, caves in Jordan, a wall in China, a town in Peru, the Colosseum Italy, and a marble building in India. These 3. ____________ have stood for a long time. If you like history, 4. ____________ just want to see beautiful things, the seven wonders might be the thing for you.

1. a. has	b. remains	c. keeps	d. comes
2. a. ancient	b. modern	c. future	d. historic
3. a. attractions	b. pyramids	c. walls	d. photographs
4. a. but	b. still	c. or	d. then

C. Multiple Choice

Circle the answer.

1. Which of the following is true?
   a. Chichen Itza Pyramid is the oldest among Seven Wonders of the Modern World.
   b. People still keep money inside Mount Hor in Jordan.
   c. The Great Wall of China isn't popular anymore.
   d. Petra is built on the highest town in the Incan world.

2. The Colosseum is all of the following BUT ...
   a. a popular place.
   b. a location hosting a famous film festival.
   c. one of the Seven Wonders of the Ancient World.
   d. in downtown Rome, Italy.

3. Why was the Great Wall of China built?
   a. to prevent people from entering China
   b. to keep treasure safe
   c. to protect people from wild animals
   d. to celebrate the victory in the war

4. What does **they** refer to in the final sentence?
   a. visitors
   b. readers
   c. attractions
   d. history

UNIT 12

The GM Debate Goes On

Have You Heard...?

For 12,000 years, people in North America have been farming and changing, one of the world's major crops — corn. Corn used to look quite different. It was smaller and harder, and maybe a different color too. To this day, corn cannot grow without people. And farmers must take part in the process of genetic modification. In America, more corn is grown than any other crop. Corn is used to make everything from soda to peanut butter.

Before We Read

A. Read and Answer

GM is short for genetic modification. Today, technology is used to change the **genes** of plants, animals, and **bacteria**. The development of GM has started one of the biggest **debates** of the 21st century. In many countries, the public seems to be amazed, but also worries about the safety of eating GM foods. Right now, ten percent of the world's **crops** are genetically **modified**. 90 percent of these crops are grown in America, Canada, and Argentina.

Write the words in bold above in the appropriate space. Change the form of the words if necessary.

	Word	Definition
1		a plant, like wheat or rice
2		to make changes
3		a thing that controls how you grow
4		discussion
5		cells that sometimes cause sickness

B. Fill in the Blanks

Complete the sentences with the words in parentheses. Change the form of the words if necessary.

1. GM is also called GE, which is short for ______________ engineering. (gene)
2. These tomatoes are ______________, so they won't go soft quickly. (modify)
3. Vinny says that ______________ modified apples taste better. (gene)
4. Do you think that genetic ______________ makes food less healthy? (modify)

C. Make Predictions

Read the first and the last paragraphs on pages 122 and 123. Answer the questions.

1. What do you think the reading is about?
   - ☐ Genetic modification is making the world hotter.
   - ☐ We are not amazed by genetic modification.
   - ☐ There are a lot of uses for genetic modification.
   - ☐ We know what is going to happen in the future.
2. What do you think the title refers to?
   - ☐ scientists taking GM tests in school
   - ☐ how much we can develop GM
   - ☐ GM and how limited this idea is
   - ☐ GM tests will be limited and unclear

GM Is Testing the Limits

Track 23

Genetic modification, or GM, is hotly debated. Supporters feel we can use it to solve a lot of the world's problems. Opponents think that we will end up causing more harm than good. Let's put the debate to the side and take a look at some of the things scientists are doing with GM.

In Japan, scientists are trying to change onions. They have made onions that won't cause you to cry when you cut them. The good news is they can change the onions, but keep the flavor.

Scientists have also been studying tomatoes. For years, they've been trying to create a tomato with a vaccine* in it. They plan to make these tomatoes into pills. These pills will be easy and cheap to produce and distribute. That way, people in poor countries will be able to afford the vaccines. Some people like this idea. However, the public worries that these vegetables will get mixed up with normal vegetables. For more safety, scientists are also growing vaccines in plants that we don't usually eat. These can still be made into cheap pills.

Scientists have not only been working on food. You may have heard of modified bacteria that can clean up oil spills. Scientists have also modified bacteria to turn soybean oil into fuel for cars. This fuel burns more cleanly, and many people are excited about it. Unfortunately, it takes a lot of land to grow the soybeans for the fuel.

Another GM product might surprise you. Scientists have added spider genes to goats! These goats produce special proteins* in their milk. The scientists hope the proteins will be as strong as spider silk. Why do they want that? Well, it turns out that spider silk is five times stronger than steel. Someday, we could have bulletproof* clothing that looks and feels like a nice silk shirt. The proteins can also be used to make fishing nets* that melt in the water. That's good news for the oceans, which are already full of garbage.

Whether you are for or against genetic modification, it's hard not to be amazed by these developments. We can only guess at what the future holds.

Reference:

* **vaccine** *medicine used to protect people from disease*
* **protein** *something found in foods and drinks which makes your body strong and healthy*
* **bulletproof** *can stop bullets*
* **fishing net** *something used to catch fish*

Comprehension Check

A. Fill in the Missing Letters

Complete the sentences with the words from the article. Change the form of the words if necessary.

1. Genetic modification is hotly **d**__________ by people all over the world.
2. Some people think GM technology will end up doing more **h**__________ than good.
3. Luckily, scientists can change the onions and keep the **f**__________ at the same time.
4. Scientists have tried to create a tomato with a **v**__________ inside.
5. Some say that the vaccine vegetables will get mixed up with **n**__________ ones.
6. Scientists can actually modify soybean oil into **f**__________ for cars.
7. Spider **g**__________ have been added to goats, so they can produce special proteins in their milk.
8. It doesn't matter if you're **f**__________ or against genetic modification. You have to admit it's interesting.

B. Classification

Match the sentence with the thing it describes.

a. modified onion	**b.** modified tomato
c. modified bacterium	**d.** modified goat

1. It is used to change soybean oil into fuel. _____
2. The item can keep you safe from illness. _____
3. This is modified by adding spider genes into it. _____
4. When you cut it, you won't get tears in your eyes. _____
5. It produces milk with special protein which is a lot stronger than it used to be. _____
6. If you have an oil spill, it will help to clean it up. _____
7. It can be made into cheap pills that are easy to distribute. _____
8. We can use proteins from this to make something to catch fish. _____

C. True or False

*Check **True** or **False**.*

	True	False
1. There's no doubt that GM can solve all the problems in the world.	☐	☐
2. Modified onions won't make people cry, and the flavor will be stronger.	☐	☐
3. Tomatoes with vaccines inside them can be made into cheap pills.	☐	☐
4. Scientists are not interested in looking at how to put vaccines in vegetables.	☐	☐
5. Fuel that is made from soybean oil is cheaper.	☐	☐
6. Spider silk is five times stronger than steel.	☐	☐
7. In the future, we'll have bulletproof silk shirts which look like normal shirts.	☐	☐
8. Fishing nets made from special proteins in goats' milk are better for the environment.	☐	☐

D. Vocabulary Building

Circle the synonym of the word/phrase in bold.

1. Air pollution has done considerable **harm** to the environment.
   a. damage   b. benefit
2. Some public holidays in Scotland are **normal** working days in England.
   a. regular   b. unusual
3. The sugar **melted** inside the cup of coffee.
   a. remained   b. dissolved
4. Everyone **was against** the new proposal.
   a. disagreed with   b. agreed with

Circle the antonym of the word/phrase in bold.

1. For your **safety**, you might want to climb with a partner.
   a. danger   b. excitement
2. Danny's mother repeatedly told him to **clean up** his apartment.
   a. mess up   b. hang up
3. We took some great pictures while in Spain, but **unfortunately** our camera got stolen.
   a. obviously   b. luckily
4. Information about the latest research findings has been **added** to the article.
   a. included   b. removed

E. Multiple Choice

Circle the answer.

1. Why is genetic modification hotly debated?
   a. Poor countries will become poorer.
   b. It won't change the balance of the environment.
   c. Some people are still questioning the benefits.
   d. Scientists are asking for more money.

2. Scientists want to create tomatoes with vaccines that ...
   a. turn bacteria into fuel for cars.
   b. produce proteins to help people live longer.
   c. are a lot harder to distribute.
   d. can be made into inexpensive pills.

3. The fourth paragraph is mainly about ...
   a. the different ways scientists are modifying bacteria.
   b. finding fuels that are cheaper than before.
   c. making the fastest cars in the world.
   d. looking for clean soybeans.

4. What will the special proteins in goats' milk be used for?
   a. to be turned into bacteria which can be used for fuel
   b. to be turned into something that can be used for fishing nets
   c. to make special goats which can produce more milk
   d. to be used to make silk shirts that melt in the water

Vocabulary Check

A. Meanings in Context

Choose the meaning of the sentence.

1. We **ended up** having to cancel our vacation.
   a. We didn't go on vacation finally.
   b. From the start, we decided not to go on vacation.

2. The government often **causes more harm than good**.
   a. It often makes things better.
   b. It often makes things worse.

3. Let's **put** that question **to the side** for now.
   a. Let's talk about that question now.
   b. Let's talk about that question later.

4. Bill always **gets mixed up with** his brother.
   a. We think Bill looks like his brother.
   b. We think they look different.

5. Nobody thought Ed could understand French. It **turns out** that he can speak it.
   a. Everyone was surprised that Ed could speak French.
   b. We all thought Ed could speak French.

6. Are you **for or against** the idea?
   a. Do you agree with the idea or not?
   b. Why don't you agree with the idea?

B. Word Definitions

Match the word with its definition.

flavor •	• a strong metal
pill •	• to have enough money to buy something
distribute •	• to become liquid
afford •	• usual
normal •	• medicine
fuel •	• gas or oil
steel •	• to give out something
melt •	• the taste of a food or drink

C. Words with Different Meanings

Match the word in bold with its definition.

1 Smoking can cause a lot of **harm** to the body. ______
This kind of soap won't **harm** your skin. ______
Definition: a *n.* damage b *v.* to damage

2 Valerie **spilled** chocolate milk on her expensive new jacket. ______
The oil **spill** is still affecting the environment. ______
Definition: a *v.* to pour by accident b *n.* something poured by accident

3 It takes a lot of **land** to raise horses. ______
The airplane **landed** ten minutes ago. ______
Definition: a *v.* to come down onto an area or space b *n.* an area or space

Reading Strategy

Compound Nouns

TIP

Compound nouns have two or more parts. The parts can be joined in several ways. Knowing what each word means also helps us better understand the meaning of a new word.

The words are written as one word.

- bullet + proof = bulletproof
- web + site = website

The words are joined with a hyphen or hyphens.

- eight-year-old
- mother-in-law

The words are written as two separate words.

- post office
- tourist attraction

• Give It a Try •

PART I

Circle the answer.

1. Which doesn't go together with **police** to make a compound noun?
   a. officer **b.** station **c.** man **d.** street
2. One word below can't be joined with **board**. Which one is it?
   a. bottle **b.** surf **c.** black **d.** key
3. Which can make a compound noun with **sales**, but we write it separately?
   a. room **b.** manager **c.** clerk **d.** person
4. Find the word that follows **book** to make a compound noun.
   a. text **b.** work **c.** case **d.** note

PART II

Choose the answer.

From my view **1.** ______________, organic foods are healthier than GM foods. I read in the **2.** ______________ that organic foods have more vitamins C, D, and E, but I don't know if it's true. I also saw a website. It explained how people who eat organic foods are less likely to get heart **3.** ______________. Some people still want to buy GM foods because they're a lot cheaper. But I don't accept this. After all, health is the most important thing.

1. **a.** place **b.** time **c.** wall **d.** point
2. **a.** television **b.** radio **c.** newspaper **d.** classroom
3. **a.** disease **b.** pain **c.** beat **d.** medicine

Further Reading

Which Apple Do You Choose?

Track 24

An apple is just an apple, right? Wrong. There are different ways to grow apples, the conventional way and the organic way.

What Does Organic Mean?

Organic farming means growing fruits and vegetables and even raising animals in an all-natural way. Organic farmers don't use man-made fertilizer* or pesticides.* They try to keep their farms clean so that the bugs won't have a place to lay their eggs. They're also not allowed to feed their animals foods grown with pesticides or give **them** drugs when they're sick. Conventional farmers can do all of these things. These things make it easier to farm, so conventional farmers can sell their products for less money.

Is Organic Food Better for You?

Some experts think that organic fruits and vegetables have no more nutritional value than conventional foods. However, the pesticides on conventional foods might cause headaches, cancer, and other health problems. Still, many say there aren't enough pesticides on conventional foods to hurt you. Others say not enough research has been done.

Organic meat is better for us in a clearer way. Conventional farmers give their animals the same medicine we take when we're sick. They give them too much medicine though. Over time, the animals' germs get used to it. Unfortunately, we also get used to it. It's possible the next time you get sick, the medicine you take might not help you.

Is It Worth It?

You have to decide for yourself if buying organic foods is worth the cost. But it's good to know that they were grown naturally. Plus, organic farming is a lot better for the environment because it keeps those chemicals out of the water and soil. Keep in mind that conventional farmers use pesticides when they're growing things like strawberries, peaches, apples, spinach, and lettuce. Try buying organically grown ones and see if you notice a difference.

Reference:

* **fertilizer** *a substance that makes plants grow*
* **pesticide** *a chemical used to kill bugs*

Comprehension Check

A. Classification

Match the sentence with the type of farming.

a. conventional farming	**b.** organic farming

1. Raise animals naturally ______
2. Use pesticides to grow crops ______
3. Give sick animals drugs ______
4. Clean farm ______

B. Fill in the Missing Letters

Complete the sentences with the words from the article. Change the form of the words if necessary.

1. Organic farmers do not feed their animals foods grown with **p**____________.
2. Some researchers believe organic fruits and vegetables do not have more **n**____________ value.
3. Pesticides found on **c**____________ foods could cause headaches, cancer, and other problems.
4. Some farmers give animals too much medicine. Eventually, the animals' **g**____________ get used to it.
5. We should decide for ourselves if buying organic foods is **w**____________ the cost.

C. Multiple Choice

Circle the answer.

1. What is conventional farming?
   a. traditional way of farming
   b. strange way of farming
   c. natural way of farming
   d. new way of farming

2. What does **them** refer to in the second paragraph?
   a. farmers
   b. pesticides
   c. drugs
   d. animals

3. Organic fruits and vegetables ...
   a. have more nutrition.
   b. cause cancer.
   c. are more natural.
   d. give us headaches.

4. Why is organic meat healthier?
   a. The animals are a lot stronger.
   b. Only experts like to eat it.
   c. It doesn't contain medicine.
   d. It doesn't have any germs.

5. Why is organic farming better for the environment?
   a. It doesn't cost a lot.
   b. It keeps chemicals out of the water and soil.
   c. It can grow more various vegetables than conventional farming.
   d. It makes vegetables grow fast.

NOTES

NOTES

AUDIO MP3 CD CONTENTS